APPETIZERS

by

Jean Paré

Dedication

To everyone who, like me, is hopelessly hooked on cookbooks.

Cover Photo

APPETIZERS

Twentieth Printing, October 1993

I.S.B.N. 0-9690695-4-5

Published and Distributed by
Company's Coming Publishing Limited
Box 8037, Station "F"
Edmonton, Alberta, Canada
T6H 4N9

**Published Simultaneously in
Canada and the United States of America**

Printed in Canada

Company's Coming Cookbooks
by Jean Paré

COMPANY'S COMING SERIES
English

HARD COVER
- JEAN PARÉ'S FAVORITES
  - Volume One

SOFT COVER
- 150 DELICIOUS SQUARES
- CASSEROLES
- MUFFINS & MORE
- SALADS
- APPETIZERS
- DESSERTS
- SOUPS & SANDWICHES
- HOLIDAY ENTERTAINING
- COOKIES
- VEGETABLES
- MAIN COURSES
- PASTA
- CAKES
- BARBECUES
- DINNERS OF THE WORLD
- LUNCHES
- PIES
- LIGHT RECIPES
- MICROWAVE COOKING
- PRESERVES *(April 1994)*

PINT SIZE BOOKS
English

SOFT COVER
- FINGER FOOD
- PARTY PLANNING
- BUFFETS

JEAN PARÉ LIVRES DE CUISINE
French

SOFT COVER
- 150 DÉLICIEUX CARRÉS
- LES CASSEROLES
- MUFFINS ET PLUS
- LES DÎNERS
- LES BARBECUES
- LES TARTES
- DÉLICES DES FÊTES
- RECETTES LÉGÈRES
- LES SALADES
- LA CUISSON AU MICRO-ONDES
- LES PÂTES
- LES CONSERVES *(avril 1994)*

table of Contents

Jean Paré was born and raised during the Great Depression in Irma, a small rural town in eastern Alberta, Canada. She grew up understanding that the combination of family, friends and home cooking is the essence of a good life. Jean learned from her mother, Ruby Elford, to appreciate good cooking and was encouraged by her father, Edward Elford, who praised even her earliest attempts. When she left home she took with her many acquired family recipes, her love of cooking and her intriguing desire to read recipe books like novels!

While raising a family of four, Jean was always busy in her kitchen preparing delicious, tasty treats and savory meals for family and friends of all ages. Her reputation flourished as the mom who would happily feed the neighborhood.

In 1963, when her children had all reached school age, Jean volunteered to cater to the 50th anniversary of the Vermilion School of Agriculture, now Lakeland College. Working out of her home, Jean prepared a dinner for over 1000 people which launched a flourishing catering operation that continued for over eighteen years. During that time she was provided with countless opportunities to test new ideas with immediate feedback – resulting in empty plates and contented customers! Whether preparing cocktail sandwiches for a house party or serving a hot meal for 1500 people, Jean Paré earned a reputation for good food, courteous service and reasonable prices.

"Why don't you write a cookbook?" Time and again, as requests for her recipes mounted, Jean was asked that question. Jean's response was to team up with her son Grant Lovig in the fall of 1980 to form Company's Coming Publishing Limited. April 14, 1981, marked the debut of "150 DELICIOUS SQUARES", the first Company's Coming cookbook in what soon would become Canada's most popular cookbook series. Jean released a new title each year for the first six years. The pace quickened and by 1987 the company had begun publishing two titles each year.

Jean Paré's operation has grown from the early days of working out of a spare bedroom in her home to operating a large and fully equipped test kitchen in Vermilion, Alberta, near the home she and her husband Larry built. Full time staff has grown steadily to include marketing personnel located in major cities across Canada plus selected U.S. markets. Home Office is located in Edmonton, Alberta where distribution, accounting and administration functions are headquartered in the company's own recently constructed 20,000 square foot facility. Company's Coming cookbooks are now distributed throughout Canada and the United States plus numerous overseas markets. Translation of the series to the Spanish and French languages began in 1990. Pint Size Books followed in 1993, offering a smaller, less expensive format focusing on more specialized topics. The recipes continued in the familiar and trusted Company's Coming style.

Jean Paré's approach to cooking has always called for easy-to-follow recipes using mostly common, affordable ingredients. Her wonderful collection of time-honored recipes, many of which are family heirlooms, is a welcome addition to any kitchen. That's why we say: "taste the tradition".

First impressions are always important but never more so than with appetizers — or, if you prefer, hors d'oeuvres, starters or even canapés. Eye appeal is a must — they should be irresistible!

First-course appetizers are usually served on a small plate at the dining table. A good rule is the heavier the meal, the lighter the appetizer. Also be sure to provide a contrast to the main course such as a seafood appetizer with a meat entreé.

Appetizers may be hot or cold, simple or elegant. Whether served from the most basic tray or elaborate chafing dish, they are always a great beginning. Sauces and dips might be served in a variety of ways, including natural containers such as a small pumpkin, cabbage, eggplant, bread loaf, grapefruit half or pineapple half. Let your imagination run wild!

When serving finger food before a meal, two or three varieties are plenty. They should be small and highly flavored. They should whet the appetite in anticipation of the next course.

Variety and quantity are substantially increased when making an entire meal of hors d'oeuvres. Try it for lunch, dinner, snack or a cocktail party.

Canapés, open-faced tidbits usually found on crackers or bread, are among the quickest appetizers. Most can be prepared ahead. Cocktail sandwiches are more time consuming and fussier but the result is always worth the effort.

Appetizers provide a great opportunity for the creative cook to be adventuresome and add flair to any meal. Read on, and you'll be ready when company's coming!

Jean Paré

PINWHEEL SANDWICHES

One of the daintiest-looking party sandwiches there is.

Sandwich loaf, sliced lengthwise, day old	1	1
Butter or margarine, softened		

Remove crusts from long bread slice. Roll lightly with rolling pin to prevent cracking when rolled. Spread with butter right to edge. Spread with filling also to edge. Starting at narrow end, roll up. Place seam side down on plate. Cover with damp tea towel and chill. To serve, cut each roll into about 12 slices. Arrange on serving plate.

PICKLE PINWHEELS: Spread bread with processed cheese spread. Lay olives, gherkins or dill pickle strips close together at narrow end. Roll. When sliced, the center will have a small slice of olive or pickle in it.

BANANA PINWHEELS: After spreading bread with butter, spread with peanut butter. Dip banana, cut the same size as bread, in pickle juice. Place on narrow edge of bread slice and roll. Chill. Slice when needed.

HAM FILLING

Cans of ham flakes	2 × 6.5 oz.	2 × 184 g
Sweet pickle relish	2 tbsp.	30 mL
Onion flakes, crushed	1 tsp.	5 mL
Salad dressing	3 tbsp.	50 mL

Combine ham, relish, onion and salad dressing. If too dry, add a bit more salad dressing. Mash with potato masher until smooth.

Pictured on page 9.

RAINBOW SANDWICHES

Here is a plateful of colors to decorate your table.

Cream cheese, softened	8 oz.	250 g
Milk	4 tsp.	20 mL
Red, green and blue food coloring		
Sliced sandwich loaf, day old	1	1
Butter or margarine, softened		

Mash cheese and milk together. Divide cheese into thirds. Mash and tint ⅓ a pleasing pink, the next green and the next blue.

Spread bread with butter. Spread ⅓ bread with pink cheese, ⅓ with green and ⅓ with blue. Stack together, covering with a fourth slice, buttered side down. Chill in a pan covered with damp tea towel until just before using. To serve, cut crusts from 4 slice sandwich. Then cut in half with hot, clean knife. Cut each half into 7. This makes 14 small oblong sandwiches for each 4 slices of bread. If you want them a little bigger, cut each half into 4. These may also be stacked with 1 more slice by using a fourth filling tinted yellow. Makes 42.

Pictured on page 9.

RIBBON SANDWICHES

Always so desirable, these are sure to whet the appetite.

Brown bread slices, day old	4	4
White bread slices, day old	2	2
Butter or margarine, softened		
Ham and egg fillings		

Use 1 white and 2 brown slices per stack. Use 2 different fillings for each stack. Place brown slices on the bottom and top. Butter and spread fillings between each slice. Cut crusts from all sides. Wrap and chill. To serve, slice in ½-inch (1 cm) slices. Then cut each slice into 3 or 4 strips. Repeat with other slices. Makes about 3½ - 5 dozen.

Pictured on page 9.

MOSAIC SANDWICHES

Make whatever shapes you like. You are limited only by the cutters you have.

Brown bread slices, day old	6	6
White bread slices, day old	6	6
Butter or margarine, softened		
Tuna filling, or other		

Cut fancy shapes out of bread slices. A doughnut cutter works providing it comes apart. Cut 2 circles from each of the bread slices making 24 circles. Cut small circles from center of 6 white and 6 brown circles. Spread solid circles with butter, then with filling. Butter circles with center holes in them. Place brown over white and white over brown with buttered side down. They can be left this way with the filling showing through the center or tiny circles can be placed in opposite colored tops — brown circle in white top and white circle in brown top. Makes 24.

TUNA FILLING

Tuna, drained	7 oz.	198 g
Finely chopped celery	¼ cup	50 mL
Onion flakes	1 tsp.	5 mL
Salt	⅛ tsp.	0.5 mL
Salad dressing	¼ cup	50 mL

Mix all ingredients together well. If dry, add more salad dressing. Makes 1 cup (250 mL).

EGG FILLING

Hard-boiled eggs, chopped	6	6
Finely diced celery	2 tbsp.	30 mL
Salt	½ tsp.	2 mL
Parsley flakes	½ tsp.	2 mL
Onion powder	¼ tsp.	1 mL
Salad dressing	¼ cup	50 mL

Mix all together. If too dry, add a bit more salad dressing. Makes about 1¾ cups (400 mL).

Pictured on page 9.

SALMON FILLING

Salmon (red is best)	7 ¾ oz.	220 g
Onion flakes	½ tsp.	2 mL
Parsley flakes	½ tsp.	2 mL
Salt	⅛ tsp.	0.5 ml
Salad dressing	¼ cup	50 mL

Remove round bones. Combine all ingredients in bowl. Add more salad dressing if too dry. Makes 1 cup (250 mL).

Pictured on page 9.

CHECKERBOARDS

Fun to make for a cocktail party.

Brown bread slices, day old	8	8
White bread slices, day old	8	8
Butter or margarine, softened		
Cream cheese filling		

Beginning with a brown slice, alternate the colors (brown, white, brown, white) buttering and spreading with filling between the slices. Make 2 stacks like this. Cut crusts from stacks. Wrap snuggly in plastic and chill about 30 minutes. Keep remaining filling soft.

Cut each stack into slices ½ inch (1 cm) thick. Spread between these ribboned slices with butter and filling. Make stacks again alternating slices so that white strips rest on brown strips, forming a checkerboard. Wrap snugly in plastic and chill. To serve, cut in ½-inch (1 cm) slices. See diagram page 150.

CREAM CHEESE FILLING

Cream cheese, softened	4 oz.	125 g
Mayonnaise	1 tbsp.	15 mL
Worcestershire sauce	1 tsp.	5 mL
Onion salt	¼ tsp.	1 mL
Yellow food coloring		

Beat all together well. Especially suited for the checkerboard sandwich since it firms and holds well when chilled. Add food coloring. Filling will be mustard color.

Pictured on page 9.

CLAM DIP

Easy does it for this seafood dip. Tasty.

Minced clams	5 oz.	142 mL
Clam juice	¼ cup	50 mL
Cream cheese, room temperature	8 oz.	250 g
Lemon juice	2 tsp.	10 mL
Worcestershire sauce	1½ tsp.	7 mL
Salt	½ tsp.	2 mL
Garlic powder	⅛ tsp.	0.5 mL

Put clams, juice and cream cheese into small bowl. Add remaining ingredients. Beat to mix well. Chill. Serve with crackers, chips or toast cups. Makes 2 cups (500 mL).

ELEGANT CLAM DIP
Double the recipe. Cut top from round or oblong loaf. Hollow out loaf leaving a shell about 1 inch (2½ cm) thick. (Reserve removed bread for dipping.) Fill with dip. Wrap in foil. Heat in 300°F (150°C) oven for 2 hours. Remove from oven and turn foil back. Cut reserved bread into dipping-size pieces. When dip is finished, break chunks from the shell for a delicious treat.

CHEESE DIP

Excellent as a vegetable dip. Equally good as a chip dip.

Envelope dry onion soup mix	½ x 1½ oz.	½ x 42.5 g
Processed cheese spread (Cheez Whiz or similar)	1 cup	250 mL
Sour cream	1 cup	250 mL
Salad dressing	1 cup	250 mL

Measure all ingredients into blender. Blend, scraping sides frequently, until thoroughly mixed. Store in refrigerator. Makes 3 cups (750 mL). Keeps about 2 weeks. Serve with chips and assorted fresh vegetables — cauliflower, broccoli, red pepper strips, green pepper strips, mushrooms, cherry tomatoes, celery.

Crab is such a gourmet treat, yet it goes so far when used as a dip like this. Quick and easy as well.

Crab, drained and membrane removed	4¾ oz.	135 g
Lemon juice	¼ cup	50 mL
Cream cheese, softened	4 oz.	125 g
Cream or milk	2-4 tbsp.	30-50 mL
Mayonnaise	2 tbsp.	30 mL
Onion salt	¼ tsp.	1 mL
Worcestershire sauce	1 tsp.	5 mL
Garlic powder (careful, not much)	⅛ tsp.	0.5 mL
Cayenne pepper	⅛ tsp.	0.5 mL

Combine crab and lemon juice in small bowl. Stir well. Allow to marinate for 30 minutes. Drain.

In medium bowl mash cheese with smallest amount of cream. Add mayonnaise, onion salt and Worcestershire sauce. Add garlic powder being careful not to add too much so as to overpower the crab flavor. Add cayenne and beat together well. Stir in crab. Now add more cream if needed. Thickness depends on how well you drained the crab. Chill. To serve, spoon into dip bowl surrounded with your favorite chips and crackers. Makes 1½ cups (375 mL).

CRAB CURRY DIP: Add ½ tsp. (2 mL) curry powder.

She thought " chicken of the sea" meant a frightened skin diver.

HOT CRAB DIP

A famous recipe. Make it ahead and pop in the oven when ready.

Cream cheese, room temperature	8 oz.	250 g
Crabmeat, drained, flaked	1½ cups	375 mL
Finely chopped onion	2 tbsp.	30 mL
Milk	2 tbsp.	30 mL
Horseradish, cream-style	½ tsp.	2 mL
Salt	¼ tsp.	1 mL
Pepper	1/16 tsp.	0.5 mL
Sliced almonds, toasted	1/3 cup	75 mL

Mash cream cheese with crabmeat. Mix in onion, milk, horseradish, salt and pepper. Spread in 9-inch (22 cm) pie plate.

Sprinkle with almonds. Bake in 375°F (190°C) oven for about 15 minutes until heated through. Keep hot on hot serving tray. Serve with crackers, chips or raw vegetables. Makes 2 cups (500 mL).

Note: A 7½ oz. (213 g) can of crab yields the above amount. However, a 5 oz. (142 g) can is sufficient to use.

SHRIMP DIP

Any chip would love to be dipped into this.

Cream cheese, softened	8 oz.	250 g
Mayonnaise	¼ cup	50 mL
Chili sauce	2 tsp.	10 mL
Lemon juice	1 tsp.	5 mL
Worcestershire sauce	1 tsp.	5 mL
Dill weed	¼ tsp.	1 mL
Garlic powder	1/16 tsp.	0.5 mL
Small or broken shrimp, rinsed and drained	4 oz.	113 g

Mash cream cheese with mayonnaise and chili sauce. Add lemon juice, Worcestershire sauce, dill and garlic. Mix well.

Add shrimp. Continue to mash and mix together until of dipping consistency. Makes 2 cups (500 mL).

Pictured in Horn Puffs, page 27.

SPINACH DIP

Served in a crusty bread shell, this makes a spectacular splash, although even served in a bowl, it will still vanish.

Frozen chopped spinach, thawed, drained and blotted dry	10 oz.	284 g
Sour cream	1 cup	250 mL
Mayonnaise	1 cup	250 mL
Chopped green onions	½ cup	125 mL
Parsley flakes	1 tsp.	5 mL
Lemon juice	1 tsp.	5 mL
Seasoned salt	½ tsp.	2 mL
Round crusty bread loaf	1	1

Put spinach, sour cream and mayonnaise into bowl. Stir. Add onion, parsley, lemon juice and seasoned salt. Mix together. Chill. Heat before serving.

Cut top from round or oblong loaf. Remove bread from the inside leaving shell about 1 inch (2½ cm) thick. (Reserve removed bread for dipping.) Fill with dip. You may need to double the recipe if the loaf is large. Wrap in foil. Heat in 300°F (150°C) oven for 2 hours. Remove from oven and turn foil back. Use reserved bread, cut into pieces, for dipping. After dip is finished break off pieces of shell and enjoy the best part of all.

Pictured on page 27.

SOUR CREAM DIP

A super quick dip with a super quick variation.

Sour cream	2 cups	500 mL
Envelope dry onion soup mix	1½ oz.	42.5 g

Stir together a few minutes before using. Chill. Makes 2 cups (500 mL). Serve with chips or vegetables.

BLUE NUTTY DIP: Add ½ cup (125 mL) crumbled blue cheese and ⅓ cup (75 mL) finely chopped pecans or walnuts. Quite different with a gentle hint of blue cheese. Add more blue cheese to taste.

AVOCADO DIP

Light and fluffy, this will win your vote.

Cream cheese	8 oz.	250 g
Ripe avocado, peeled and mashed	1	1
Mayonnaise	½ cup	125 mL
Lemon juice	1½ tbsp.	25 mL
Garlic powder	⅛ tsp.	0.5 mL

Paprika

Have cream cheese at room temperature. Beat cheese, mashed avocado, mayonnaise, lemon juice and garlic powder together well. Spoon into small bowl.

Sprinkle paprika over top. Serve as a dip with fresh raw vegetables, corn chips, tortilla chips, etc. Makes 2½ cups (625 mL).

BEST VEGETABLE DIP

Make up this large recipe, use half and freeze half. Ready to take with you or to use at a moment's notice. A sweeter than usual vegetable dip.

Cream cheese, softened	8 oz.	250 g
Corn syrup, light or dark	½ cup	125 mL
Granulated sugar	½ cup	125 mL
Salad oil	1 cup	250 mL
Vinegar	¼ cup	50 mL
Minced onion flakes (or use 3 times as much minced fresh onion)	¼ cup	50 mL
Lemon juice	1 tbsp.	15 mL
Dry mustard powder	1 tsp.	5 mL
Celery seed	1 tsp.	5 mL
Salt	½ tsp.	2 mL
Paprika	¼ tsp.	1 mL

Put cream cheese, syrup and sugar into mixing bowl. Dark syrup adds a bit more color to finished product. Beat well. Add salad oil and mix. Add remaining ingredients. Beat until blended. Chill. Serve with assorted raw vegetables — mushrooms, broccoli, green pepper strips, cauliflower, celery. Makes 3 cups (750 mL).

About the best all-round never-get-tired-of dip you will find. A good spur-of-the-moment choice. Equally good with vegetables or chips. A real standby.

Mayonnaise	1 cup	250 mL
Sour cream	1 cup	250 mL
Dry onion flakes	2 tsp.	10 mL
Dry parsley flakes	2 tsp.	10 mL
Dry dill weed	2 tsp.	10 mL
Seasoned salt	1 tsp.	5 mL
Monosodium glutamate (optional)	1 tsp.	5 mL

Mix all ingredients in bowl. Chill. Serve with potato chips, broccoli, cauliflower, mushrooms, celery sticks, carrot sticks, bread sticks, radish, cherry tomatoes, green pepper slices and any other vegetable you can think of. Makes 2 cups (500 mL).

BLUE CHEESE DIP

One of the best blue cheese dips going! Get the fresh vegetables ready.

Cream cheese	8 oz.	250 g
Blue cheese	4 oz.	113 g
Sour cream (or more to thin)	1 cup	250 mL
Worcestershire sauce	1 tbsp.	15 mL
Dry onion flakes, crushed	1 tsp.	5 mL

Have cheeses at room temperature. Mash both together with fork. Mix in remaining ingredients. Transfer to small bowl. Beat with electric beater until fluffy or use blender. Serve with chips or vegetables. Makes 2½ cups (625 mL).

CHAFING DISH SAUCES

Pour one of these over your favorite meatballs. Try a different one every time.

CHILI GRAPE SAUCE

Chili sauce	1¼ cups	300 mL
Grape jelly	1 cup	250 mL
Lemon juice	1 tsp.	5 mL

Mix in saucepan. Pour over meatballs. Makes 2¼ cups (550 mL) deep grape-colored sauce.

PEANUT SAUCE

Peanut butter	¼ cup	50 mL
Water	½ cup	125 mL
Brown sugar	2 tbsp.	30 mL
Soy sauce	1 tbsp.	15 mL
Lemon juice	2 tsp.	10 mL
Crushed red chili peppers	½ tsp.	2 mL
Garlic powder (or 1 clove minced)	¼ tsp.	1 mL

Mix in saucepan. Simmer 5 minutes. Pour over Satay, see page 83, in chafing dish. Makes ¾ cup (175 mL).

SWEET AND SOUR DARK

Water	½ cup	125 mL
Vinegar	½ cup	125 mL
Brown sugar, packed	1 cup	250 mL
Cornstarch	4 tsp.	20 mL

Heat in saucepan. Pour over meatballs. Makes 1 ¼ cups (340 mL) dark sauce.

TOMATO CHILI SAUCE

Canned tomatoes	2 x 14 oz.	2 x 398 mL
Chili powder	2 tsp.	10 mL
Salt	1 tsp.	5 mL

Heat in saucepan. Pour over meatballs. Makes ¾ cups (175 mL) red sauce.

TOMATO SAUCE

Tomato sauce	7½ oz.	213 mL
Ketchup	½ cup	125 mL
Sweet pickle relish	2 tbsp.	30 mL
Brown sugar	2 tbsp.	30 mL
Vinegar	1 tbsp.	15 mL
Onion flakes	2 tsp.	10 mL
Worcestershire sauce	1 tsp.	5 mL

Heat in saucepan. Pour over meatballs. Makes 2 cups (500 mL) red sauce.

Pictured on page 63.

MUSHROOM CHEESE SAUCE

Condensed cream of mushroom soup	10 oz.	284 mL
Cream cheese	8 oz.	250 g
Milk	½ cup	125 mL

Heat and pour over meatballs. Makes 2½ cups (625 mL).

Pictured on page 63.

SWEET AND SOUR LIGHT

Granulated sugar	1 cup	250 mL
Water	¾ cup	175 mL
Vinegar	¾ cup	175 mL
Cornstarch	2 tbsp.	30 mL
Paprika	1 tsp.	5 mL
Salt	½ tsp.	2 mL

Heat, stirring, until boiling. Pour over meatballs. Makes 1¾ cups (425 mL) light colored sauce.

Pictured on page 63.

RED SWEET SAUCE

Chili sauce	1 cup	250 mL
Mild molasses	¼ cup	50 mL
Vinegar	¼ cup	50 mL

Heat and pour over meatballs. Makes 1½ cups (300 mL) reddish black sauce.

MUSHROOM BARBECUE SAUCE

Condensed cream of mushroom soup	10 oz.	284 mL
Soup can full of barbecue sauce	10 oz.	284 mL

Heat and pour over meatballs. Makes 2 ¼ cups (550 mL) reddish orange sauce.

STROGANOFF SAUCE

Water	1¼ cups	300 mL
Cornstarch	4 tsp.	25 mL
Instant beef-in-a-mug soup powder	1 tbsp.	15 mL
Sliced mushrooms, fried	¼ cup	50 mL
Sour cream	⅔ cup	175 mL

Heat, stirring, until boiling. Pour over meatballs. Makes 2 cups (500 mL) creamy mushroom colored sauce.

SEAFOOD SAUCE

A great dip or sauce for all your seafood needs.

Chili Sauce	½ cup	125 mL
Ketchup	¼ cup	50 mL
Sweet pickle relish	3 tbsp.	50 mL
Horseradish	½ tsp.	2 mL
Worcestershire sauce	½ tsp.	2 mL

Mix all ingredients in bowl. Chill. To serve, put into small bowl for dipping. Makes about 1 cup (225 mL).

You know you are at a firefly race when you hear "On your mark, get set, glow!"

TARTAR DILL SAUCE

Good for mushroom dipping, fish dipping, actually just good.

Mayonnaise	¾ cup	175 mL
Sweet pickle relish	¼ cup	50 mL
Lemon juice	1 tbsp.	15 mL
Dry dill weed	½ tsp.	2 mL

Mix all ingredients. Any French-fried food is good dipped in this sauce. Makes 1 cup (250 mL).

PINEAPPLE SAUCE

You will love the tangy taste, as a meat dip and as a fruit dip.

Pineapple juice	¼ cup	50 mL
Cornstarch	2 tbsp.	30 mL
Vinegar	¼ cup	50 mL
Granulated sugar	¼ cup	50 mL

Put pineapple juice, cornstarch, vinegar and sugar into small saucepan. While stirring, bring to boil over medium heat to thicken. Excellent as a fruit dip and also for dipping meat such as chicken wings. Makes about ½ cup (125 mL). Double the recipe if serving many people.

PLUM SAUCE

Sauce will be dark or light depending on whether you use regular plum or greengage jam.

Plum jam	1 cup	250 mL
Cider vinegar	3 tbsp.	50 mL
Granulated sugar	2 tsp.	10 mL

Stir all 3 ingredients together. If mixture contains a lot of skins, put through a sieve. Serve with egg rolls or as a dip for any kind of meat. Makes 1 generous cup (250 mL).

Pictured on page 63.

SURPRISE CANAPÉS

A smash hit when children are among the guests! Serve the adults first to be sure they get a taste.

White bread slices, 1 or 2 days old	6	6
Butter	½ cup	125 mL
Peanut butter (smooth)	½ cup	125 mL
Dry, fine bread crumbs		

Cut off crusts, then cut into ½-inch (1 cm) strips. Place on baking sheet. Bake in 350°F (180°C) oven for about 15 minutes until toasted and browned.

Melt butter and peanut butter in heavy saucepan. Using tongs, dip toasted strips in mixture. Don't soak them. Place on waxed paper to cool for 30 minutes.

Put some crumbs in plastic or paper bag. Add a few bread strips. Shake to coat. Store in airtight container. Makes 4 dozen.

Variation: Use graham cracker crumbs instead of bread crumbs.

Pictured on page 27.

BLUE CHEESE WAFERS

Crisp and nutty with only a slight hint of blue cheese. Excellent.

Grated sharp Cheddar cheese	1 cup	250 mL
Butter or margarine, softened	½ cup	125 mL
Crumbled Blue cheese	⅓ cup	75 mL
All-purpose flour	1½ cups	375 mL
Seasoned salt	1½ tsp.	7 mL
Finely chopped walnuts	⅓ cup	75 mL

Mix cheese with butter. Add rest of ingredients. Shape into rolls about 1½ inches (3.5 cm) in diameter. Chill. Slice about ¼ inch (1 cm) thick. Arrange on ungreased baking sheet. Bake in 375°F (190°C) oven for about 10 minutes until firm and slightly browned. Makes about 6 dozen.

Pictured on page 27.

CHEESE CRISPS

You won't go wrong by doubling the recipe. Crunchy little tidbits.

Butter or margarine, softened	½ cup	125 mL
Grated Cheddar cheese	1 cup	250 mL
All-purpose flour	1 cup	250 mL
Salt	½ tsp.	2 mL
Cayenne pepper	¼ tsp.	1 mL
Crisp rice cereal	1 cup	250 mL

Cream butter and cheese together well. Mix in flour, salt and cayenne pepper. Cayenne may be doubled if preferred.

Add rice cereal and work into batter. Roll into small balls and arrange on ungreased baking sheet. Press with fork. Bake in 350°F (180°C) oven for 12 to 15 minutes until lightly browned. Makes about 4 dozen.

CHEESE NUT CRISPS: Add ¼ cup (50 mL) chopped nuts to batter.

Pictured on page 27.

HAM AND CHEESE ROLLS

So handy to have in the freezer.

White sandwich loaves, sliced	1½	1½
Thin ham slices	18	18
Thin cheese slices	18	18
Asparagus tips	12 oz.	341 mL
Butter, soft or melted		

Cut crusts from bread slices. Roll with rolling pin. Lay slice of cheese on the bread then a slice of ham. Lay asparagus spear along edge. Roll. Brush with butter. Freeze on tray and store in plastic bag. To serve, cut each roll into 3 pieces. Bake in 400°F (200°C) oven for about 10 minutes until toasted. Broil briefly, if needed to assist in toasting. Makes 54.

ASPARAGUS CHEESE ROLL: Omit ham slices.

ASPARAGUS HAM ROLL: Omit cheese slices.

PARTY RYE ROUNDS

Good on any kind of bread. So last-minute easy.

Loaf of rye bread, sliced	1	1
Medium onion, very finely chopped	1	1
Mayonnaise	1 cup	250 mL
Grated Parmesan cheese	½ cup	125 mL
Prepared mustard	½ tsp.	2 mL

Toast 1 side of bread under broiler on second shelf down from heat. Remove from heat.

Mix onion, mayonnaise, cheese and mustard together. Spread on untoasted side of bread. Broil until bubbly and puffy. Cut into quarters to serve. Makes 5 dozen.

Variation: Bread may be spread with filling, baked in 400°F (200°C) oven for about 10 minutes. Very good.

Variation: Instead of chopped onion, use very thin slices of mild onion to put on bread. Cover with mayonnaise-cheese-mustard mixture. Broil until bubbly and browned.

SPEEDY CRACKERS: Omit mustard. Add ½ tsp. (2 mL) Worcestershire sauce. Spoon onto party crackers. Broil until bubbly and browned. Don't turn your back on them or they will burn. Makes 3 dozen.

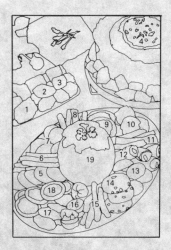

These festive morsels are tender and light. A sure-fire hit.

Grated Cheddar cheese, softened	1½ cups	375 mL
Butter or margarine, softened	½ cup	125 mL
Egg	1	1
Onion powder	¼ tsp.	2 mL
Dry mustard powder	½ tsp.	2 mL
Sandwich loaf, sliced	1	1

Put cheese, butter, egg, onion powder and mustard into mixing bowl. Beat together until smooth and soft.

Spread 2 slices of bread with cheese mixture. Stack together and cover with third slice. Cut off crusts. Cut sandwich into quarters either forming squares or triangles. Spread all sides, except bottom, with cheese mixture. Repeat with rest of slices. Place on foil-lined baking sheet. Freeze. Store in plastic bag. To serve, place on foil-lined baking sheet. Bake in 350°F (180°C) oven for about 10 minutes until browned. Serve hot. Makes 5 dozen.

EASY PUFF DELIGHTS: Beat until very light and fluffy, 1½ cup (375 mL) shredded Cheddar cheese (softened) and ¾ cup (175 mL) butter or margarine. Spread on bread slices and proceed as above.

CHEESE BOXES: Serve this as a contrast to Puff Delights. Makes a zippy spread.

Grated Cheddar cheese, softened	2 cups	500 mL
Mayonnaise	1 cup	250 mL
Worcestershire sauce	1 tbsp.	15 mL
Prepared mustard	1 tsp.	5 mL
Onion powder	¼ tsp.	1 mL
Salt	¼ tsp.	1 mL

Beat together well and proceed as for Puff Delights.

Pictured on page 27.

CHEESE CUBES

You will love them hot and enjoy the leftovers cold — if there are any.

White bread loaf, unsliced	1	1
Butter or margarine	½ cup	125 mL
Grated sharp Cheddar cheese	1 cup	250 mL
Cream cheese	4 oz.	125 g
Egg whites, beaten stiff	2	2

Cut crusts from bread loaf. Cut into 1-inch (2.5 cm) cubes. Set aside.

Put butter, Cheddar and cream cheese into top of double boiler. Melt, stirring frequently. Remove from heat.

Fold beaten egg whites into cheese mixture. Dip bread cubes into cheese mixture to coat all sides. This is easier to do if you use a fork to pierce each cube before dipping. Freezing the bread cubes first makes it easier yet. Use a knife to help spread if needed. Place on ungreased baking sheet. Chill in refrigerator overnight. Bake in 400°F (200°C) oven for about 10 minutes until golden brown. After chilling overnight, these may be frozen on tray, then stored in plastic bag. Thaw before baking. Makes about 5 dozen.

Variation: Use Swiss cheese instead of Cheddar for a lighter color and milder flavor.

Pictured on page 27.

If everyone drove a pink car, we would have a pink-car-nation.

PUFFED STRAWS

If only all straw tasted this good!

Puff pastry	14 oz.	397 g
Grated Parmesan cheese	1 cup	250 mL
Paprika	½ tsp.	2 mL

Roll half of the pastry at a time into a square about 10 x 10 inches (25 x 25 cm).

Mix cheese with paprika. Sprinkle ¼ over top of ½ of rolled pastry. Fold other half over cheese. Roll until original size. Sprinkle with ¼ cheese mixture. Press cheese into pastry a bit. Cut down center of pastry, then cut into strips about ½ inch (1 cm) wide. Transfer to ungreased baking sheet. Repeat with second ½ of pastry. Bake in 350°F (180°C) oven for about 15 minutes until nicely browned. Makes 40.

Variation: Use grated Cheddar cheese instead of Parmesan.

Pictured on page 27.

PARMESAN STICKS

A great snack that can be stored by the tinful.

White bread slices (or brown, or both)	12	12
Butter or margarine, melted	1 cup	250 mL
Grated Parmesan cheese	1½ cups	375 mL

Remove bread crusts. Cut each slice into 4 to 5 strips. Brush each strip generously with melted butter. Dip in bowl of Parmesan cheese. Place on greased baking sheet. Bake in 350°F (180°C) oven for about 15 minutes. Check often as they brown quickly. Serve hot or cold. Makes 48 to 60.

SESAME STICKS: Dip buttered strips in sesame seeds instead of Parmesan cheese. These are really good.

CHEESE STRIPS: Dip 1 side of strip in butter, then in grated Cheddar. Place cheese side up on greased baking sheet. Bake in 400°F (200°C) oven for 8 - 10 minutes. These are best served warm. Makes 4 or 5 dozen.

CHEESE PENCIL STICKS

Crispy-browned, a bowlful of these won't be enough.

Commercial cheese spread	½ cup	125 mL
Butter or margarine, softened	½ cup	125 mL
All-purpose flour	1¼ cups	300 mL
Salt	½ tsp.	2 mL
Cayenne pepper (optional)	¼ tsp.	1 mL

Combine all ingredients. Use a cookie press or roll into long rope. Cut into short pieces about 3 inches (8 cm) long. Arrange on ungreased baking sheet. Bake in 400°F (200°C) oven for 8 to 10 minutes until firm and lightly browned. Makes about 7 dozen pencil-slim sticks.

PARMESAN PENCILS: Exchange ¾ cup (175 mL) grated Parmesan cheese for the cheese spread.

Pictured on page 27.

PUFF SHELLS

Puff shells have long ranked high as one of the most elegant ways to serve food.

Water	1 cup	250 mL
Butter or margarine	½ cup	125 mL
All-purpose flour	1 cup	250 mL
Salt	¼ tsp.	1 mL
Eggs	4	4

Measure water and butter into saucepan. Bring to boil.

Add flour and salt. Stir vigorously until mixture leaves sides of pan and forms a ball. Remove from heat.

Add eggs, 1 at a time, beating well after each addition. Drop small spoonfuls of batter on ungreased baking sheet. Bake in 400°F (200°C) oven for about 15 minutes until puffed, brown and dry. Transfer to rack and cool. Makes 48 to 60, depending on how bite-size you want them to be.

Pictured on page 27.

Accompany these with a soft cheese, such as Brie or Camembert, for easy spreading.

All-purpose flour	2 cups	500 mL
Granulated sugar	½ cup	125 mL
Baking powder	2 tsp.	10 mL
Salt	½ tsp.	2 mL
Nutmeg	¼ tsp.	1 mL
Cinammon	¼ tsp.	1 mL
Butter or margarine	½ cup	125 mL
Currants	½ cup	125 mL
Mixed peel, finely chopped	¼ cup	50 mL
Egg, beaten slightly	1	1
Milk	⅓ cup	75 mL

In large bowl put flour, sugar, baking powder, salt, nutmeg and cinammon. Cut in butter until crumbly.

Stir in currants and peel.

Add eggs and milk. Stir to form ball of dough. Roll ¼ inch (⅔ cm) thick on floured surface. Cut into 2 or 3-inch (5 or 7.5 cm) rounds. Fry in frying pan over medium heat browning both sides. Pan should be lower temperature than for cooking pancakes. Serve cold. Makes 2 or 3 dozen.

Pictured on page 27.

Any owl with laryngitis doesn't give a hoot.

PIE CRUST PASTRY

For quiches, meat pies, turnovers, sausage rolls or even small rounds.

All-purpose flour	5 cups	1.15 L
Salt	2 tsp.	10 mL
Baking powder	1 tsp.	5 mL
Brown sugar	3 tbsp.	45 mL
Lard, room temperature	1 lb.	454 g
Egg	1	1
Vinegar	2 tbsp.	30 mL
Add cold water to make	1 cup	225 mL

Measure flour, salt, baking powder and brown sugar into large bowl. Stir to distribute all ingredients.

Add lard. Cut into pieces with knife. With pastry cutter, cut in lard until whole mixture is crumbly and feels moist.

Break egg into measuring cup. Beat well with fork. Add vinegar. Add cold water to measure 1 cup (225 mL). Pour slowly over flour mixture stirring with fork to distribute. With hands, work until it will hold together. Divide into 4 equal parts. Wrap in plastic and store in refrigerator for 1 or 2 weeks. Store in freezer to have a continuing supply. Makes 6-8 crusts.

Hog wash isn't exactly a pig's laundry.

TOAST POINTS

Makes a nice variation for your favorite spread or pâté.

Trim crusts from square bread slices. Toast 1 side only of each slice under broiler until light brown. Cut each slice down the center making 2 rectangle shapes. Cut each rectangle cornerwise making 4 elongated triangles. These are toast points. Spread filling on untoasted side. Broil 6 or 7 inches (15 - 17 cm) from heat about 5 minutes or until bubbly hot.

TOAST SQUARES: Cut each slice into 4 squares rather than triangles.

TOASTED ROUNDS: Slice small loaf, such as a submarine bun, into round slices. Toast or leave plain.

TOAST TRIANGLES: Cut each slice into 4 triangles by cutting diagonally from corner to corner.

TOAST CUPS

These tiny cups add flair to your favorite fillings. So easy to make and store. Make lots.

White bread slices	12	12

Cut crusts from sandwich loaf bread slices or other type loaf. Cut each slice into 4 squares. Press into small ungreased muffin cups. A small empty muffin cup that holds 4 tsp. (20 mL) is a good size. Bake in 350°F (180°C) oven on bottom rack for about 15 minutes until corners are well browned. Turn pan over to remove toast cups. Cool completely. Store in plastic bag. To serve, fill with your favorite filling or pile cups around filling for self service. Makes 48.

Variation: Butter 1 side of bread square before pressing into pan. Keep buttered side up.

HORN PUFFS

Lend a special party feeling to your tray of goodies. These are good with regular pastry too.

Puff pastry (or pie crust pastry)
Egg, beaten

Roll out pastry fairly thin. Cut into long, narrow strips. These can be ¼ inch (½ cm) wide or a bit wider. Dampen 1 edge of strip. Wind strips around metal cream horns, overlapping and pressing to seal as you go. For tiny horns, wind only half way. Brush with egg, arrange on baking sheet. Bake in 425°F (220°C) oven for about 15 minutes until browned. Let stand for 5 minutes. Push off metal cases. Cool. Stuff with lobster filling, ham, cheese or filling of your choice. Try Shrimp Dip, page 16, and garnish with red pepper or pimiento.

Pictured on page 27.

LAST MINUTE KABOBS

Some ideas for making a few, or unlimited little hors d'oeuvres. Easy to serve on toothpicks.

Stuffed olive
Pineapple chunk
Ham cube

Orange section
Ham cube
Pineapple chunk

Maraschino cherry
Cheese cube
Ham cube

Stuffed olive
Small shrimp
Orange section

Stuffed olive
Ham cube
  (or other)
Pickled onion

Maraschino cherry
Pineapple chunk
Ham cube
  (or other)

Orange section
Maraschino cherry
Pineapple chunk

Tiny cooked sausage
Pineapple chunk
Tiny cooked sausage

Stuffed olive
Small shrimp
Pineapple chunk

Small shrimp
Small mushroom
Small shrimp

Apple wedge
  (brown sugared)
Tiny cooked
  sausage
Apple wedge
  (brown sugared)

Pineapple chunk
Stuffed olive
Cheese cube

Stuffed olive
Pickled onion
Roast beef cube

Maraschino cherry
Small shrimp
Pineapple chunk

A several-bite finger food that the whole crowd will love.

All-purpose flour	1½ cups	375 mL
Granulated sugar	1 tbsp.	15 mL
Baking powder	1 tbsp.	15 mL
Salt	½ tsp.	2 mL
Cooking oil	¼ cup	50 mL
Milk	½ cup	125 mL

Combine flour, sugar, baking powder and salt in bowl. Stir well.

Add oil and milk. Mix into ball, adding a bit more milk if needed to make a soft dough. Roll about ¼ inch (1 cm) thick on lightly floured board. Cut into 2½ inch (6 cm) rounds. Cover with topping and bake. Makes 18.

TOPPING

Tomato sauce	3 tbsp.	50 mL
Oregano, sprinkle		
Pepperoni slices (optional)	54 - 72	54 - 72
Mozzarella cheese slices, quartered	5	5
(or use shredded)		

Spread ½ tsp. (2 mL) tomato sauce over each pizza followed with a sprinkle of oregano. Put about 3 to 4 slices of pepperoni on each. Top with mozzarella cheese. Arrange on ungreased baking pan. Bake in 400° F (200° C) oven for 10 to 12 minutes until browned.

Pictured on page 27.

If an athlete gets athlete's foot, does an astronaut get missle toe?

PIZZA IN MINIATURE

Good for all ages. Add your own extras whether it be green peppers, olives, mushrooms, or Parmesan cheese or leave as is.

English muffins	**6**	**6**
Tomato paste	**5 ½ oz.**	**156 mL**
Oregano	**½ tsp.**	**2 mL**
Salt	**½ tsp.**	**2 mL**
Onion salt	**¼ tsp.**	**1 mL**
Sliced pepperoni, smokies or summer sausage		
Sliced Mozzarella cheese, or shredded		

Split muffins. Arrange on baking sheet.

In small bowl combine tomato paste, oregano, salt and onion salt. Spread over top of buns.

Slice pepperoni fairly thin. Put 4 slices on each bun half. Cover with cheese. A mozzarella cheese slice can be cut in quarters. Bake in 400°F (200°C) oven for about 10 minutes until hot and cheese has melted. Cut each into quarters. Serve hot. Makes 4 dozen.

PIZZA BUBBLES: Flatten refrigerator biscuits to fit muffin cups. Press up sides as well. Spread with tomato sauce mixture and put at least one meat slice on top covered with cheese. Bake in 425°F (220°C) oven for about 10 minutes until browned. These will be like a bun with filling rolled inside. It produces a larger snack. Makes 10.

PIZZA ON RYE: Use rye bread slices instead of English muffins.

PIZZA CRACKERS: Use round crackers (Ritz works well). Spread with ¼ tsp. (1 mL) tomato sauce. Sprinkle with whole oregano. Ground oregano may be used but it won't show up as well. Sprinkle a few shreds (as fine as you can shred them) of Cheddar cheese over top. Just a few, so oregano can be seen also. Bake in 350°F (180°C) oven for 10 minutes. allow to cool and dry thoroughly. Store in cookie tin, plastic bag or freezer.

Pictured on page 27.

The choice is open to your imagination. Especially handy when you have no idea of quantity needed. Just make them as required.

CUCUMBER SNACK: Spread salad dressing on round cracker. Score cucumber with fork or peel it. Slice and place 1 slice on top of salad dressing. Sprinkle with salt and pepper if desired. Make a few at a time as required. A wee dab of sour cream on top goes well.

SHRIMP SNACK: Put a dab of chili sauce or seafood sauce on round cracker. Put a cocktail shrimp in center. So easy to keep a can of cocktail shrimp on hand.

EGG SNACK: Spread a round cracker with salad dressing. Slice a hard-boiled egg and place 1 slice on top. Add a light sprinkle of salt and pepper if desired. A dab of salad dressing on top is optional.

SMOKED OYSTER SNACK: Put a dab of chili sauce or seafood sauce on round cracker. Cut smoked oysters in half. Place 1 piece on top.

CHEESE SNACK: Slice small cheese roll and place on round cracker. Good with a bit of salad dressing also.

CHEESE ONION SNACK: Put slice of small cheese roll on round cracker. Cut small pickled onion in half and put flat side down in center of cheese.

RADISH SNACK: Cut radish in half. Slice each half quite thin almost to the bottom. Press a bit to make radish-half fan-like. Place on round cracker alone or with a bit of mayonnaise. If radish is large, cut into single slices and use 1 slice per cracker.

A camel without a hump could be named Humphry.

CHEESE NUT PINWHEELS

These little cheese rolls have a pleasant nutty flavor. They make a tiny taste treat.

FILLING

Cream cheese, room temperature	4 oz.	125 mL
Shredded sharp Cheddar cheese	¼ cup	50 mL
Chopped pecans or walnuts	¼ cup	50 mL
Mayonnaise	1 tbsp.	15 mL
Lemon juice	1 tsp.	5 mL
Onion flakes	1 tsp.	5 mL
Worcestershire sauce	¼ tsp.	1 mL

Mix all 7 ingredients together in bowl. Set aside.

PASTRY

All-purpose flour	1 cup	250 mL
Baking powder	2 tsp.	10 mL
Granulated sugar	1 tbsp.	15 mL
Salt	½ tsp.	2 mL
Cooking oil	3 tbsp.	50 mL
Cold water	¼ cup	50 mL

Measure first 4 ingredients into bowl. Stir to mix.

Add oil and water. Stir until mixture forms a ball, adding a bit more water if needed to make a soft dough. Turn out onto lightly floured surface. Pat or roll to form 9 X 12-inch (22 X 30 cm) rectangle. Spread with filling. Starting at wide edge, roll up, pinching edge to seal. Chill for at least 1 hour. Slice about ¼ inch (½ cm) thick. Place cut side down on greased baking sheet. Bake in 400°F (200°C) oven for about 10 minutes until golden brown. Makes about 3 dozen.

Pictured on page 27.

QUICK CHEESE BITES

So easy, so cheesy, so pleasing!

Butter or margarine	½ cup	125 mL
Blue cheese	4 oz.	125 g
Cans of refrigerator biscuits	2	2

Melt butter and cheese in heavy saucepan over medium-low heat, stirring frequently.

Cut each biscuit into 4 pieces. Dip each piece into butter-cheese mixture. Arrange on greased baking sheet. Bake in 450°F (220°C) oven for about 10 minutes until puffed and browned. Better warm but may be served hot or cold. Makes 40.

Variation: Place quartered biscuits into 2 greased, round 8-inch (20 cm) pans. Pour melted mixture over top. Move pieces around lightly to coat all of them. Bake in 400°F (200°C) oven for about 10 minutes or until golden brown. Good.

Pictured on page 27.

CHEESE NUGGETS

You will be taking more bites than you expected after you try these bite-size treats.

Butter	½ cup	125 mL
All-purpose flour	1 cup	250 mL
Grated sharp Cheddar cheese	2 cups	500 mL
Cayenne pepper	¼ tsp.	1 mL

Mix butter and flour together well. Add cheese and work in well. Shape into small marble-size balls. Place on ungreased baking sheet. Bake in 375°F (190°C) oven for about 10 minutes. Makes 36.

Pictured on page 27.

CRACKER SNACKER

A snap to make. The bacon fat makes the cracker seem like pastry.

Soda crackers	24	24
Bacon slices, cut in half crosswise	12	12

Wrap each cracker with bacon. Arrange on ungreased baking sheet with sides, putting overlapping side down. Bake in 350°F (180°C) oven for 10 to 15 minutes until golden brown. Serve hot. Makes 24.

PIZZA SHORTBREAD

A tasty little savory snack.

All-purpose flour	2 cups	500 mL
Butter or margarine	1 cup	250 mL
Grated Cheddar cheese	½ cup	125 mL
Grated Parmesan cheese	¼ cup	50 mL
Finely chopped pimiento (optional, but colorful)	2 tbsp.	30 mL
Salt	¼ tsp.	1 mL
Oregano	½ tsp.	2 mL
Paprika		

Mix flour and butter. Add Cheddar and Parmesan cheeses. Stir in salt and oregano. Shape into long roll or 2 short rolls. Chill 1 hour. Slice about ¼ inch (1 cm) thick. Arrange on ungreased baking sheet leaving room for expansion. May also be rolled in balls and pressed with fork.

Sprinkle with paprika. Bake in 375°F (190°C) oven for about 10 minutes or until golden brown. Makes about 2½ dozen.

SIMPLE STUFFED MUSHROOMS

There aren't many ingredients to assemble. Try the variations, especially the Blue-Stuffed.

Medium mushrooms	**12-16**	**12-16**
Butter or margarine	**¼ cup**	**50 mL**
Mushroom stems, chopped		
Finely chopped onion	**¼ cup**	**50 mL**
Salt	**¼ tsp.**	**1 mL**
Pepper	**⅛ tsp.**	**0.5 mL**
Dry bread crumbs	**½ cup**	**125 mL**

Remove stems from mushrooms. Arrange caps on baking tray.

Put butter, stems, onion, salt and pepper in frying pan. Fry slowly until onions are clear and soft.

Stir in bread crumbs. Stuff caps. Bake in 350°F (180°C) oven for about 10-15 minutes or broil for about 5 minutes. Serve hot. Makes 12-16.

BLUE-STUFFED MUSHROOMS: Add ¼ cup (50 mL) crumbled blue cheese with crumbs. Very tasty.

SWISS-STUFFED MUSHROOMS: Add ½ cup (125 mL) shredded Swiss cheese with crumbs.

CHEDDAR-STUFFED MUSHROOMS: Add ½ cup (125 mL) grated Cheddar cheese with crumbs.

PARMESAN-STUFFED MUSHROOMS: Add ½ cup (125 mL) grated Parmesan cheese with crumbs. Add ⅛ tsp. (0.5 mL) oregano (optional) or add ⅛ tsp. (0.5 mL) poultry seasoning.

Pictured on page 117.

MUSHROOM ROLLS

This hors d'oeuvre is a favorite — you'll eat until it's gone.

Chopped onion	½ cup	125 mL
Mushrooms, chopped	½ lb.	250 g
Butter or margarine	¼ cup	50 mL
Cream cheese	8 oz.	250 g
Worcestershire sauce	½ tsp.	2 mL
Salt	½ tsp.	2 mL
Pepper	⅛ tsp.	0.5 mL
Garlic powder	⅛ tsp.	0.5 mL
Loaf of white sandwich bread, sliced	1	1
Butter or margarine for brushing		

Put onion, mushrooms and butter into frying pan. Sauté until soft and onions are clear.

Add cream cheese in chunks. Add next 4 ingredients. Stir until cheese melts. Let stand until completely cool.

Remove crusts from bread. Roll each slice with rolling pin. Spread mushroom mixture on each slice and roll up as for jelly roll. Brush with melted or soft butter. Place on tray to freeze. Store in plastic bag. To serve, cut each roll into 3 pieces. Arrange on ungreased baking sheet. Bake in 400°F (200°C) oven for 10 to 15 minutes until toasted and hot. Makes 4 dozen.

JIFFY MUSHROOM ROLLS:
Spread undiluted cream of mushroom soup on each slice. Roll. Cut into 3 pieces. Wrap each with ½ slice of half-cooked bacon, securing with toothpick. Broil turning once until bacon is cooked. Serve hot.

1. Citrus Cocktail page 70
2. Mock Peach Daiquiri page 69
3. Orange Julius page 70
4. Mock Pink Lady page 68
5. Fruit Platter page 66
   a. Cantaloupe
   b. Kiwifruit
   c. Apple
   d. Strawberries
   e. Honeydew
6. Easy Fruit Dip page 67
7. Fresh Fruit Cocktail page 67
8. Fruit Sauce page 67

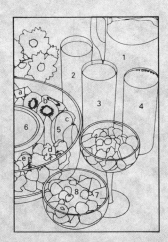

POLYNESIAN MUSHROOMS

These have the appearance of being stuffed with meat. Delicious.

Medium mushrooms	18	18
Butter or margarine	¼ cup	50 mL
Garlic powder (or 1 clove, minced)	¼ tsp.	1 mL
Shredded Monterey Jack cheese	¼ cup	50 mL
Mushroom stems, finely chopped		
Milk	2 tbsp.	30 mL
Soy sauce	1 tsp.	5 mL
Dry bread crumbs	½ cup	125 mL

Gently remove stems from mushrooms.

In small saucepan over medium heat combine butter, garlic powder, cheese, mushroom stems, milk, soy sauce and crumbs. Stir well to melt butter. Fill caps. Arrange on baking sheet. Broil for 3-4 minutes. Serve hot. Makes 18.

Pictured on page 117.

SEAFOOD MUSHROOMS

Two favorite seafoods combine to make this exotic dish.

Cream cheese, softened	4 oz.	125 g
Butter or margarine, softened	½ cup	125 mL
Horseradish	1 tbsp.	15 mL
Garlic salt	1 tsp.	5 mL
Shrimp, rinsed and drained	4 oz.	113 g
Crab, membrane removed	4¾ oz.	135 g
Large mushrooms, stems removed	24	24

Put cheese, butter, horseradish and garlic salt into mixing bowl. Beat until light and smooth.

Add shrimp and crab. Beat together well.

Stuff mushrooms. Place on baking sheet. Bake in 350°F (180°C) oven for about 15 minutes until filling begins to get a bit crusty. Makes 24.

MUSHROOM TURNOVERS

One of the tastiest appetizers ever. May be frozen baked or un-baked. Absolutely delectable.

CREAM CHEESE PASTRY

Cream cheese	8 oz.	250 g
Butter or margarine	½ cup	125 mL
All-purpose flour	1½ cups	375 mL

Have cheese and butter at room temperature. Put into bowl and beat together well. Mix in flour. Shape into ball. Chill at least 1 hour.

FILLING

Butter or margarine	3 tbsp.	50 mL
Large onion, finely chopped	1	1
Fresh mushrooms, chopped	½ lb.	250 g
All-purpose flour	2 tbsp.	30 mL
Salt	1 tsp.	5 mL
Pepper	¼ tsp.	1 mL
Thyme	¼ tsp.	1 mL
Sour cream	¼ cup	50 mL
Egg, beaten	1	1

Combine butter, onion and mushrooms in frying pan. Sauté about 10 minutes until tender.

Add flour, salt, pepper and thyme. Stir together. Add sour cream. Stir until thickened. Remove from heat. Cool thoroughly.

Roll pastry fairly thin. Cut into 3-inch (7½ cm) rounds. Place 1 tsp. (5 mL) filling in center of each circle. Dampen outer half edge with beaten egg. Fold over and press edges together with fork or fingers to seal. Arrange on greased baking sheet. Cut tiny slits in top of each.

Brush tops with beaten egg. Bake in 450°F (230°C) oven for about 10 minutes or until golden brown. Makes 3 to 4 dozen.

Note: To use canned sliced mushrooms rather than fresh, drain and chop 2 - 10 oz. (284 mL) cans and add to onion. Just as delicious and always on hand.

(continued on next page)

To freeze ahead: Do not brush with egg. Freeze on tray. Transfer frozen turnovers to carton or plastic bag. Before serving, arrange on greased baking sheet. Brush with egg. Prick holes in tops. Bake in 350°F (180°C) oven for about 20 to 30 minutes until browned. If already cooked heat in 325°F (160°C) oven for 15-20 minutes until hot.

MUSHROOM CUPS: Fill toast cups with mushroom filling. Heat in 400°F (200°C) oven for about 10 minutes or until bubbly hot.

Pictured on page 117.

FAVORITE MUSHROOMS

One of the best. Hold in refrigerator until ready to broil.

Mushrooms, medium large	**24**	**24**
Butter or margarine	**3 tbsp.**	**50 mL**
Finely chopped onion	**1 cup**	**250 mL**
Ground beef	**¼ lb.**	**115 g**
Finely chopped celery	**2 tbsp.**	**30 mL**
Mushroom stems, finely chopped		
Ketchup	**¼ cup**	**50 mL**
Dry bread crumbs	**¼ cup**	**50 mL**
Garlic powder	**1 tsp.**	**5 mL**
Salt	**½ tsp.**	**2 mL**
Pepper	**½ tsp.**	**2 mL**
Grated Parmesan cheese	**¼ cup**	**50 mL**
Grated mozzarella cheese (optional)	**½ cup**	**125 mL**

Remove stems from mushrooms with a gentle twist. Reserve.

Melt butter in frying pan. Add onion, ground beef and celery. Fry until onions are clear and soft and beef is nicely browned.

Add next 6 ingredients. Stir well. Remove from heat. Stuff mushroom caps. Arrange on baking sheet.

Sprinkle with Parmesan cheese, then with mozzarella, if you wish. Place on second rack from broiler. Broil for about 5 minutes, until heated through. Serve hot. Makes 24.

Note: If using small mushrooms, omit mozzarella or place only a few shreds on each cap, otherwise it will topple off.

Pictured on page 117.

CRAB-STUFFED MUSHROOMS

Serve as finger food or as a table appetizer. Succulent.

Bite-size mushrooms	40	40
Butter or margarine	1 tbsp.	15 mL
All-purpose flour	2 tsp.	10 mL
Rich milk	¼ cup	50 mL
Lemon juice	1 tbsp.	15 mL
Salad dressing	1 tbsp.	15 mL
Shredded Cheddar cheese	¼ cup	50 mL
Crab, membrane removed	4¾ oz.	135 g
Onion flakes, crushed	1 tsp.	5 mL

Remove mushroom stems, reserve for another purpose.

Melt butter in saucepan. Stir in flour. Add milk, lemon juice and salad dressing stirring until it boils and thickens.

Add cheese. Stir to melt. Stir in crab and onion. Fill mushroom caps. Bake in 400°F (200°C) oven for 15 to 20 minutes until heated through. Makes about 40 finger hors d'oeuvres.

Pictured on page 117.

SPINACH-STUFFED MUSHROOMS

The shredded Cheddar spruces up the looks of these.

Frozen chopped spinach, barely cooked and drained	10 oz.	284 g
Sour cream	½ cup	125 mL
Tomato sauce	¼ cup	50 mL
Grated Cheddar cheese	1 cup	250 mL
Butter or margarine, melted	3 tbsp.	50 mL
Garlic salt	⅛ tsp.	0.5 mL
Large, fresh mushrooms	12	12

Mix spinach, sour cream, tomato sauce and cheese. Set aside.

Combine butter and garlic salt. Remove mushroom stems. Dip caps in butter, place in baking pan. Stuff with spinach mixture. Bake in 350°F (180°C) oven for 10 to 15 minutes. Makes 12 large caps.

Pictured on page 117.

Easy and showy little bites. Cool cooking!

Cucumber, long and narrow	1	1
Salad dressing	½ cup	125 mL
Sour cream	¼ cup	50 mL
Grated carrot	2 tbsp.	30 mL
Finely chopped radish	2 tsp.	10 mL
Parsley flakes	¼ tsp.	1 mL
Salt, sprinkle		
Pepper, sprinkle		

Score cucumber peel all around with fork tines from top to bottom. Peel if you would rather. Slice into ½-inch (1½ cm) slices. Using tip of small spoon scoop out center of each slice about half way down from top.

Mix salad dressing, sour cream, carrot, radish and parsley. Sprinkle with salt and pepper. Stir and fill hollows in slices. Makes ¾ cup (175 mL).

STUFFED CUCUMBER

Remove from refrigerator, slice and serve. A cool canapé.

Straight cucumber	1	1
Cream cheese, softened	4 oz.	125 g
Dry onion flakes, crushed	½ tsp.	2 mL
Dried dill weed	½ tsp.	2 mL
Paprika		

Score cucumber all around by scraping from top to bottom with fork tines. Cut ends off and scoop out seeds from center. A small spoon and a vegetable corer work well. Be sure to remove all seeds because that is the part where most of the moisture is.

Mash cheese with a fork. Add onion and dill. Mash together. Stuff cucumber. Wrap and chill.

To serve, slice and sprinkle with paprika. May be served as is or on a cracker.

STUFFED CELERY

There are so many stuffings, besides the usual cheese spread, to use with celery. Stuffing stalks before cutting speeds up process. Chill. To serve, cut in short sections either on the square or on the diagonal.

CHEESE STUFFING

Jar of cheese spread	1	1

Stuff celery stalks. Chill until ready to serve.

SHRIMP STUFFING

Broken shrimp, drained	4 oz.	113 g
Cream cheese	4 oz.	125 g
Finely chopped pimiento	1 tbsp.	15 mL
Finely chopped nuts	1 tbsp.	15 mL
Lemon juice	1 tsp.	5 mL
Worcestershire sauce	¼ tsp.	1 mL
Parsley flakes	¼ tsp.	1 mL
Onion salt	¼ tsp.	1 mL

Mix together well. Stuff celery stalks. Just excellent. Makes 1 cup (250 mL).

COTTAGE CHEESE STUFFING

Cottage cheese, drained	½ cup	125 mL
Salad dressing	1 tbsp.	15 mL
Prepared mustard	¼ tsp.	1 mL
Paprika for sprinkling		

Mix first 3 ingredients. Stuff celery. Sprinkle with paprika. Makes 1 cup (250 mL).

PEANUT BUTTER STUFFING

Cream cheese, softened	4 oz.	125 g
Smooth peanut butter	2 tbsp.	30 mL
Curry powder	¼ tsp.	1 mL
Onion powder	¼ tsp.	1 mL

Mix together and stuff celery. Crushed peanuts make a good sprinkle. Also chopped pimiento and pimiento cheese are good additions. Makes ½ cup (125 mL).

(continued on next page)

APRICOT STUFFING

Cream cheese, softened	4 oz.	125 g
Apricot jam	2 tbsp.	30 mL
Curry powder	1 tsp.	5 mL

Mix together. Stuff celery. Makes ½ cup (125 mL).

CHUTNEY STUFFING

Use chutney instead of apricot jam in Apricot Stuffing.

OLIVE STUFFING

Cream cheese, softened	4 oz.	125 g
Ketchup	2 tbsp.	30 mL
Very finely chopped pecans or walnuts	2 tbsp.	30 mL
Stuffed green olives, finely chopped	5	5

Mix all together. Stuff celery. Makes ⅔ cup (175 mL).

PINEAPPLE STUFFING

Cream cheese	4 oz.	125 g
Crushed pineapple, drained	¼ cup	50 mL
Horseradish (optional)	1 tsp.	5 mL

Mix together. Stuff celery. Makes ⅔ cup (175 mL).

CREAM CHEESE STUFFING

Cream cheese	4 oz.	125 g
Mayonnaise	1 tbsp.	15 mL
Worcestershire sauce	1 tsp.	5 mL
Onion salt	¼ tsp.	1 mL
Caviar (optional)		

Mix first 4 ingredients together. Stuff celery. Sprinkle caviar over top if desired. Makes ½ cup (125 mL).

NUT STUFFING: Add ½ cup (125 mL) chopped nuts to cream cheese mixture. Omit caviar.

CELERY FLOWERS: Using several stalks, fill with cheese spread, cream cheese, shrimp stuffing, apricot stuffing, or your choice. Beginning with smaller stalks, reshape to resemble original bunch of celery, adding more stuffing to hold together. Wrap snuggly in waxed paper and chill. To serve, slice thinly into flowers.

STUFFED CHERRY TOMATOES

These elegant showpieces can be filled with so many different fillings. As well as these below, use other spreads or use mushroom stuffings.

Cherry tomatoes	**2 cups**	**500 mL**

Cut tops from tomatoes. Scoop out some of the pulp. Sprinkle inside with salt. Invert tomatoes upside down to drain for ½ hour. Top may be used as a lid after stuffing tomato. Or tomato may be cut almost to the bottom to make 4 or 6 petals. Use Rice Filling, sandwich fillings or spreads.

RICE FILLING

Cooked rice	1 cup	250 mL
Green onion, finely chopped	1-2	1-2
Chopped nuts (optional)	1 tbsp.	15 mL
Worcestershire sauce	⅛ tsp.	0.5 mL
Salad dressing	1 tbsp.	15 mL

Combine ingredients. Add more salad dressing if needed. Overstuff tomatoes. Replace tops.

Naturally oceans roar. You would too if you found lobsters in your bed.

Although there are several steps to this, it really is easy to do. Makes a delicious, mild pasta first course.

Cooked medium egg noodles or linguini or your favorite pasta	3 cups	750 mL
Sliced fresh mushrooms	1 cup	250 mL
Butter or margarine	1 tbsp.	15 mL
Whipping cream	1 cup	250 mL
Butter	2 tbsp.	30 mL
White wine (optional but good)	2 tbsp.	30 mL
Grated Parmesan cheese	¼ cup	50 mL
Salt and pepper to sprinkle		
Parsley		
Nutmeg		

Cook pasta according to package directions.

Sauté mushrooms in butter until tender.

Heat cream and butter in saucepan until boiling. Reduce heat and simmer very slowly for no more than 2 minutes. Stir in wine.

Drain noodles. Toss with mushrooms, sauce and cheese. Sprinkle with salt and pepper. Divide among 6 small plates. Sprinkle with parsley and nutmeg. Serve immediately. Makes 6 sit-down appetizers.

You know that Martians are metric if they say "Take me to your Litre".

LITTLE LATKES

Serve this well known European snack soon. Different and very economical.

Medium potatoes, peeled and shredded	4	4
Eggs, beaten	2	2
Onion flakes	2 tsp.	10 mL
All-purpose flour	1 tbsp.	15 mL
Salt	1 tsp.	5 mL
Lemon juice	1 tsp.	5 mL
Baking powder	1 tsp.	5 mL

Shred potatoes and set aside.

Beat eggs in bowl until frothy. Add onion, flour, salt, lemon juice and baking powder. Drain juice from potatoes and stir potatoes into egg mixture. Drop by small spoonfuls into well-greased frying pan. Brown on both sides. May be reheated in 350°F (180°C) oven for about 10 minutes until hot. Serve sour cream or apple sauce for dipping. Makes about 5 dozen 1½-inch (4 cm) latkes.

Pictured on page 27.

POTATO SKINS

A nifty hors d'oeuvre or a great sit-down table appetizer when rice or noodles are being served with the main course.

Medium potatoes, baked and cooled	6	6
Butter or margarine, melted	6 tbsp.	100 mL
Shredded Cheddar cheese	¾ cup	175 mL
Bacon bits	½ cup	125 mL
Sour cream	¾ cup	175 mL

Cut each potato into 4 lengthwise sections. Scoop out pulp leaving a shell ¼ inch (½ cm) thick. Don't leave shell too thick or it won't be crisp enough. Brush shells on both sides with melted butter. Arrange on ungreased baking sheet. Bake in 350°F (180°C) oven for 10 to 12 minutes. Remove from oven. Sprinkle with Cheddar cheese and bacon bits. Return to oven for 2 to 3 minutes until cheese melts.

(continued on next page)

Plop a dollop of sour cream on each piece to serve. Makes 24 hors d'oeuvres or serve 4 sections per plate to 6 appreciative guests.

Variation: Cheddar cheese and bacon bits may be replaced by a sprinkle of Parmesan cheese, onion salt or garlic salt. Skins may also be cut in shorter pieces 1 inch (2½ cm) wide. Smaller pieces are served with a sour cream and chive mixture for a dip. This is excellent finger food.

DEEP-FRIED POTATO SKINS

Everybody loves to dip these in their favorite sauce.

Large potatoes, baked and cooled	6	6
All-purpose flour	⅓ cup	75 mL
Seasoned salt (or salt, pepper and paprika)	1 tsp.	5 mL
Fat for deep-frying		

Cut potatoes in half lengthwise. Scoop out center of potato leaving a shell about ¼ inch (½ cm) thick. Cut shells crosswise into pieces about 1 inch (2½ cm) wide.

Coat with flour. Deep-fry in hot fat 375°F (190°C) for about 2 minutes until light brown. Remove to paper towels to drain.

Sprinkle with seasoned salt. Serve with sour cream and chives. Try other sauces too. Serve warm. Makes 5 dozen.

Note: These may be deep-fried ahead and reheated later. Heat in 400°F (200°C) oven for 5 to 10 minutes until hot.

POTATO PEELINGS: Cut clean peelings into finger length strips. Brush with melted butter or margarine. Arrange skin side down on baking sheet. Bake in 400°F (200°C) oven for about 15 minutes until cooked and crisp. Serve warm with sour cream.

MEATLESS SAMOSAS

Not too heavily spiced, these are really good. Dream of mystic India while you sample.

Salad oil	1 tbsp.	15 mL
Medium onion, chopped	1	1
Chopped celery	¼ cup	50 mL
Ginger	1 tsp.	5 mL
Garlic powder	1 tsp.	5 mL
Chili powder	¼ tsp.	1 mL
Mashed potatoes	1 cup	250 mL
Cooked peas	¾ cup	175 mL
Egg roll wrappers	1 pkg.	1 pkg.

Fat for deep-frying

Combine oil, onion and celery in frying pan. Fry until browned. Add ginger, garlic powder and chili powder. Cook and stir for about 2 minutes. Stir in potatoes and peas. Cool.

Cut egg roll wrappers diagonally into 4 triangles. Put about 1 tbsp. (15 mL) or less, of mixture in center of each. Moisten edges with water. Fold over. Press to seal. Fry in 375°F (190°C) fat until golden brown. Turn once to brown both sides. To reheat, place on baking sheet in 350°F (180°C) oven for 10 to minutes until hot.

Note: Wonton wrappers may be used although they are a bit thinner.

Note: These may be baked in 450°F (230°C) oven for about 10 minutes. They won't be as crispy brown as when deep-fried.

WATER CHESTNUTS

A Hawaiian treat.

Water chestnuts, drained	10 oz.	284 mL
Soy sauce	¼ cup	50 mL
Granulated sugar	¼ cup	50 mL
Bacon slices, half cooked or raw, cut in half crosswise	8	8

(continued on next page)

Marinate chestnuts in soy sauce for 30 minutes to 1 hour. Stir often to distribute.

Remove chestnuts and roll in sugar.

Wrap bacon around chestnut, securing with toothpick. Arrange on baking sheet. Bake in 400°F (200°C) oven for 10-20 minutes until bacon is cooked. May also be broiled. Makes 16.

Variation: Roll in brown sugar for a treat. Sugar may be omitted entirely if preferred.

EGG ROLLS

Easier to make than you think. A scrumptious appetizer.

Thinly sliced cabbage	3 cups	750 mL
Thinly sliced celery	1 cup	250 mL
Bean sprouts (fresh is best)	2 cups	500 mL
Bamboo shoots, drained	19 oz.	540 mL
Cooked pork, finely chopped	½ lb.	250 g
Shrimp, drained and chopped	4 oz.	113 g
Chopped green onions	½ cup	125 mL
Soy sauce	2 tbsp.	30 mL
Granulated sugar	1 tsp.	5 mL
Salt	½ tsp.	2 mL
Garlic powder (or clove, minced)	¼ tsp.	1 mL
Pepper	⅛ tsp.	0.5 mL
Egg roll skins	16	16
Fat for deep-frying		

Boil cabbage and celery in boiling, salted water in separate saucepans until tender crisp. The cabbage will cook sooner, thus the need for separate pans. Drain. Rinse with cold water. Drain again.

Combine next 10 ingredients in large bowl. Stir well. Add cooled cabbage and celery. Mix.

A. Place 3 tbsp. (50 mL) filling near 1 corner of egg roll skin.
B. Fold corner over filling, tucking it in snuggly.
C. Fold side corner toward center.
D. Roll over once more.
E. Fold flap over. Moisten edges with water to seal. See page 149 for picture method. Deep-fry, seam side down, turning once, until browned. Serve hot with Plum Sauce, page 23, or Sweet and Sour Light, page 21. Makes about 16.

FRENCH-FRIED VEGETABLES

Practically a whole meal could be made of these. Vegetables are listed below, followed by various batters. While batter may be used alone, vegetables are especially good when both battered and crumbed. When battered only, the finished product is smooth. When battered and crumbed, the result is a browner, crumbly textured look. For a thin coating, no batter is used, just crumbs or flour. You will discover your favorite by trying them all. These batters are used for meat, poultry and seafood too.

Broccoli: Cut into florets. Boil in salted water for about 5 minutes. Do not overcook because it will be too difficult to handle. Drain. Cool.

Carrots: Cut into finger strips. Boil in salted water until tender-crisp. Drain. Cool.

Cauliflower: Cut into florets. Boil in salted water about 5 minutes. Do not overcook because it won't handle well. Drain. Cool.

Celery: Cut into finger strips. Boil in salted water about 5 minutes. Drain. Cool.

Green Peppers: Cut into strips or rings. Do not cook.

Mushrooms: Use bite-size if possible. Do not cook.

Onions: Cut into ¼-inch (1½ cm) slices. Separate into rings. Do not cook.

Parsnips: Cut into finger strips. Boil in salted water until tender-crisp. Drain. Cool.

Sweet Potatoes: Cut into 2 or 3-bite-size pieces. Boil in salted water until tender-crisp. Drain. Cool.

Zucchini: Cut into wedges about 2½ inches (6 cm) long and about ½ inch (1 cm) wide. Do not cook.

Pictured on page 117.

IT'S A CINCH BATTER

This is easy, fool proof and it stays crisp.

Pancake mix	1 cup	250 mL
Water	1 cup	250 mL

Dry bread crumbs, finely rolled (optional)

Fat for deep-frying

Spoon-beat pancake mix and water together until mixed well. Dip food. Roll in crumbs if desired. Deep-fry at 375°F (190°C).

CRISPY BATTER

This favorite coating retains its crispness for a lengthy spell.

All-purpose flour	¾ cup	175 mL
Cornstarch	¼ cup	50 mL
Baking powder	2 tsp.	10 mL
Salt	1 tsp.	5 mL
Water	¾ cup	175 mL

Dry bread crumbs, finely rolled (optional)

Fat for deep frying

Measure first 4 ingredients into bowl. Stir to mix.

Add water. Spoon-beat until smooth. You probably will need to add a bit more water if too stiff to coat well. Dip food. Coat with crumbs if desired. Deep-fry at 375°F (190°C).

CRUMB COATING

This thin coating browns quickly to give a dark appetizing look.

Egg, beaten	1	1
Dry bread crumbs, finely rolled		

Fat for deep-frying

Dip food in egg, roll or shake in crumbs and deep-fry at 375°F (190°C).

BARELY COATED

This simple dipping gives a thin covering but it is sufficient for zucchini and mushrooms.

Milk	⅓ cup	75 mL
Chicken Shake-and-Bake, Regular or Mexican style	1 pkg.	1 pkg.

Dip zucchini in milk, then in Shake-and-Bake. Deep-fry at 375°F (190°C). Tasty and easy.

FLOUR COATING

Use this when a seasoned thin coating is preferred.

All-purpose flour	⅓ cup	75 mL
Salt	1 tsp.	5 mL
Pepper	¼ tsp.	1 mL
Garlic powder	¼ tsp.	1 mL
Paprika	¼ tsp.	1 mL
Cayenne pepper	⅛-¼ tsp.	0.5-1 mL

Fat for deep-frying

Measure all ingredients into bowl. Mix well. Dredge damp food in mixture. Deep-fry at 375°F (190°C).

Variation: Use finely rolled crumbs rather than flour. Stir frequently because spices tend to sink to the bottom.

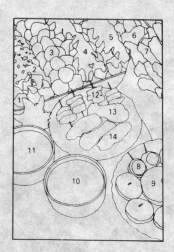

VEGETABLE MARINADE

Quantities are approximate and can be varied as can the vegetables. A very popular hors d'oeuvre.

Small cauliflower	1	1
Broccoli florets	3 cups	750 mL
Cherry tomatoes	2 cups	500 mL
Celery, cut in sticks	2 cups	500 mL
Carrots, cut in sticks	3	3
Mushrooms, fresh or canned	2 cups	500 mL
Green pepper, cut in strips or rings	1	1
Italian dressing	1 cup	250 mL

Divide cauliflower into bite-size pieces. Do the same with broccoli leaving some stem. Add tomatoes whole. Cut celery and carrots into sticks. Add mushrooms. Cut green pepper in strips or rings. Put into container with tight-fitting cover. Pour Italian dressing over all. Put cover on. Shake to distribute dressing. Chill overnight turning container occasionally. Drain. Serve. Makes 12 cups (3 L).

VEGETABLE PLATTER

You don't have to be on a diet to enjoy this all-time favorite.

Cauliflower, cut into florets
Broccoli, cut into florets
Green pepper, cut into strips or rings
Carrot sticks
Radishes, plain or cut into roses
Celery sticks
Mushrooms
Cherry tomatoes

Arrange several vegetables according to color for variety. Put bowl of dip in center or 2 or 3 bowls of dip beside platter. Serve with Dilly Dip, page 19, or any others you would like to try.

FRUIT PLATTER

Start a holiday right by entertaining for breakfast. A melon platter is a showy item. Prepare several kinds of fruit.

Canteloupe
Honeydew
Watermelon
Strawberries
Apple slices (dip in lemon juice)
Papaya, if in season
Mango, if in season
Kiwifruit

Cut melons into small wedges or into balls. Leave strawberries whole. Peel kiwifruit and slice. Slice and dip apple. Arrange on platter. Supply serving spoon for guests to help themselves.

Variation: Serve with picks and Fruit Sauce, page 67, so guests can nibble while the next course is being prepared. Easy Fruit Dip, page 67, and Caramel Fruit Sauce, page 67, are excellent.

Pictured on page 45.

FRUIT COCKTAIL

A good combination which is so easy to have ready ahead of time.

Mandarin orange segments, drained	10 oz.	284 mL
Fruit cocktail with juice	14 oz.	398 mL
Grapefruit sections, reserve juice	14 oz.	398 mL
Kiwifruit	1	1
Maraschino cherries	6	6

Put orange segments, fruit cocktail with juice and grapefruit sections into bowl. Stir lightly to mix. Add some grapefruit juice if it seems to need more. Spoon into 6 sherbets. You will have too much fruit. Use the rest another day.

Peel kiwifruit. Slice. Cut each slice in half. Place 1 piece on top of fruit on the side. Place 1 cherry in center of each sherbet. Makes 6.

Fresh fruit, tastefully sauced, is a delicious appetizer. Fruit may be varied according to the season, or make a last minute combination from the shelf.

Red and/or green grapes
Orange sections
Pineapple chunks, canned or fresh
Banana, sliced
Strawberries, cut up
Pear, peeled and cubed
Raspberries
Blueberries

Use a minimum of 3 kinds of fruit for variety. Fill sherbets or fruit nappies. Spoon sauce over top.

FRUIT SAUCE

Cream cheese, softened	8 oz.	250 g
Granulated sugar, syrup or honey	¼ cup	50 mL
Orange juice	½ cup	125 mL

Beat all ingredients together. Add more orange juice if needed to thin sauce a bit more, although there will be some juice on the fruit so don't make it too thin. Really good. Makes a scant 2 cups (450 mL).

EASY FRUIT DIP

Plain yogurt	1 cup	250 mL
Icing (confectioner's) sugar	3 tbsp.	50 mL
Grated lemon peel	½ tsp.	2 mL

Combine all ingredients. A bit less lemon peel may be used. This makes a yummy dip for any fruit. Makes 1 cup (250 mL).

CARAMEL FRUIT DIP

Sour cream	1 cup	250 mL
Brown sugar	1 tbsp.	15 mL
Kahlua	1 tbsp.	15 mL

Stir together. If you prefer to omit kahlua, add more brown sugar to taste. Make a good supply. It vanishes in no time. Makes 1 cup (250 mL).

Pictured on page 45.

MOCK PINK LADY

A great aperitif! Pink and smooth.

Cream or homo milk	1½ cups	375 mL
Lemon juice	2 tbsp.	30 mL
Grenadine	1 tbsp.	15 mL
Granulated sugar	1 tbsp.	15 mL
Ice cubes	6	6

Measure cream, lemon juice, grenadine, sugar, and ice cubes into blender. Blend until ice is gone. Serve immediately. Makes 3 cups (750 mL) including foam.

Pictured on page 45.

If there is one thing worse than raining cats and dogs, it's hailing taxis.

An aperitif with lots of body to it.

Peaches, drained, reserve juice	14 oz.	398 mL
Lemon juice	1 tbsp.	15 mL
Ice cubes	6	6
Homo milk	⅓ cup	75 mL
Peach juice	½ cup	125 mL
Rum flavoring	½ tsp.	2 mL

Put peaches, lemon juice, ice cubes, milk, peach juice and rum flavoring into blender. Blend until ice is gone. Serve immediately. Makes 2½ cups (575 mL) including foam.

Note: Fresh peaches may be used. Add 1 tbsp. (15 mL) granulated sugar or to taste.

MOCK STRAWBERRY DAIQUIRI: Use fresh strawberries instead of peaches. Add 1 tbsp. (15 mL) granulated sugar or to taste.

Pictured on page 45.

Of course you know that bride and groom spiders are known as newly webs.

CITRUS COCKTAIL

A quick and easy refreshing drink. Mild but not sweet.

Frozen concentrated lemonade	6 oz.	170 g
Frozen concentrated orange juice	6 oz.	170 g
Club soda	5 cups	1.25 L
Ginger ale	5 cups	1.25 L

Combine lemonade and orange juice. Add club soda and ginger ale. Stir gently. Pour into juice glasses. Makes 18, 5 oz. (135 mL) drinks.

Pictured on page 45.

ORANGE JULIUS

A favorite before-meal or anytime drink for young and old alike.

Frozen concentrated orange juice	6 oz.	170 g
Milk	1 cup	250 mL
Water	1 cup	250 mL
Egg (optional)	1	1
Granulated sugar	2 tbsp.	30 mL
Vanilla	2 tsp.	10 mL
Ice cubes	12	12

Put orange concentrate into blender. Add next 5 ingredients. May be made this far ahead of time. To serve, add ice cubes. Blend until ice is gone. Serve immediately. Makes 5 cups (1.25 L).

Pictured on page 45.

TOMATO JUICE COCKTAIL

Zip up the tomato juice for a variation.

Tomato juice	19 oz.	540 mL
Lemon juice	1 tsp.	5 mL
Worcestershire sauce	½ tsp.	2 mL
Onion salt	¼ tsp.	1 mL
Celery salt	⅛ tsp.	0.5 mL
Pepper	⅛ tsp.	0.5 mL

Pour tomato juice into pitcher. Add rest of ingredients. Stir well. Cover and chill. Stir before pouring. Serves 4 to 5.

CHERRY ROLLS

If an hors d'oeuvre can be cute, then this is the one. So tiny, so pretty, it cheers any plate of morsels.

Bacon slices, cut in half lengthwise and crosswise	**4**	**4**
Maraschino cherries	**12**	**12**

Fry bacon until clear and still soft. Do not cook completely or it won't roll when cool. Cut each slice into 3 sections. Wrap around cherries securing with toothpicks. Chill. To serve, heat in 400°F (200°C) oven for 5 minutes or until bacon is sizzling. Serve hot. Makes 12.

Pictured on cover.

DATES AND BACON

Hard to imagine how good these are.

Bacon slices, half-cooked	**8**	**8**
Pitted dates	**24**	**24**

Depending on length of bacon slices, cut crosswise into 2 or 3 pieces. Wrap bacon around date, securing with toothpick. Place in shallow baking pan. Bake in 350°F (180°C) oven for about 15 minutes or until bacon is cooked. May also be broiled. Makes 24.

PINEAPPLE BACON: Use pineapple chunks instead of dates. Very good.

If you want to see a moth dance, go to a moth ball.

DATE COVERS

Put these on a fruit tray for a surprise.

Grated sharp Cheddar cheese	2 cups	500 mL
Butter or margarine, softened	½ cup	125 mL
All-purpose flour	1 cup	250 mL
Cayenne pepper	¼ tsp.	1 mL
Pitted whole dates	36	36
Pecan halves	36	36

Put cheese and butter into bowl. Mix together well. Add flour and pepper. Mix well until a ball is formed.

Put a pecan half into each date. Shape a small piece of dough around each stuffed date to enclose it. Arrange on ungreased baking sheet. Bake in 375°F (190°C) oven for about 12 minutes or until browned. Makes 2½ - 3 dozen.

Variation: These may be made using dates only and omitting pecans.

PICKLE PASTRIES: Use Cream Cheese Pastry (page 48). Roll out into small rounds. Lay thin pickle slice on round. Dampen edge. Cover with second round. Brush with milk or beaten egg. Prick hole in top. Bake in 400°F (200°C) oven for 10 minutes until brown. Makes 3 dozen.

PICKLE FANCIES: Enclose olive, gherkin or pickled onion in pastry. Bake in 375°F (190°C) oven for about 12 minutes until browned.

If you see a cow wearing a crown, you will know it's a dairy queen.

Curry lovers are free to add more curry, but these are really scrumptious as they are. A treat from India.

Cooking oil	1 tbsp.	15 mL
Medium onion, chopped	1	1
Ginger	1 tsp.	5 mL
Garlic powder	1 tsp.	5 mL
Curry powder	1 tsp.	5 mL
Ground beef	1 lb.	500 g
Tomato, chopped (optional)	1	1
Cooked peas, frozen or fresh	¾ cup	175 mL
Egg roll wrappers	1 pkg.	1 pkg.

Fat for deep frying

Put oil and onion into frying pan. Fry until browned. Add ginger, garlic powder and curry powder. Cook and stir for about 2 minutes. Add ground beef and tomato and scramble-fry. Stir in peas. Allow to cool.

Cut egg roll wrappers diagonally into 4 triangles. Put about 1 tbsp. (15 mL), or less, of mixture in center. Moisten edges with water. Fold over and press to seal. Fry in 375°F (190°C) fat until golden brown, turning once. To reheat, place on baking sheet in 350°F (180°C) oven for 10 to 15 minutes or until hot. Makes about 5 dozen.

Note: Wonton skins may be used. They are a bit thinner.

Note: May be baked in 450°F (230°C) oven for about 10 minutes. They don't get as bubbly-brown in the oven as when deep-fried.

A frog has an easy life. It eats whatever bugs it.

SAUSAGE ROLLS

A bit fussy to make but when you see how much everyone enjoys them it will all be worthwhile.

Skinless sausages, about 16 to a pound, (450 g) or sausage meat	16	16
Pie crust or puff pastry, your own or a mix		

Fry sausages slowly to remove fat and also to cook. Drain well and cool. This can be done a day ahead. Sausage meat can be used by forming into sausage-shaped rolls with hands dipped in cold water to help keep from sticking. Fry as for sausages. Cool thoroughly.

Roll out pastry on floured surface. Lay a sausage on outer edge. Trim edge even. Cut strip the width of sausage. Roll sausage up in pastry, allow extra for overlap, and cut pastry. Dampen overlap to seal. Cut wrapped sausage in half and place on baking tray, sealed side down. Repeat with remaining sausages. When cut in half you have a 2 bite-size piece. They may be left whole if a larger snack is desired. Place on ungreased baking tray. Bake in 400°F (200°C) oven for about 20 minutes until browned. Cool. Store in container in refrigerator. Makes 32.

To serve: Arrange on baking tray. Heat in 400°F (200°C) oven for about 10 minutes until hot. May be heated in microwave although crust won't be quite as crisp.

Pictured on cover.

SAUSAGE BALLS

It is difficult to choose a favorite between these variations.

Sausage meat	1 lb.	454 g
Chopped onion	¾ cup	175 mL
Chopped celery	⅓ cup	75 mL
Brown sugar	2 tbsp.	30 mL
Cider vinegar	2 tbsp.	30 mL
Chili sauce	½ cup	125 mL

(continued on next page)

Shape sausage meat into tiny balls.

Put onion, celery, sugar, vinegar and chili sauce into saucepan large enough to hold meatballs in single layer. Bring onion mixture to boil. Cover and simmer 5 minutes. Add meatballs. Bring to boil again. Simmer 10 to 15 minutes more. Serve hot with picks. Makes 4 dozen.

SAUSAGE BALL FRIES: Dredge balls in Regular Chicken Shake and Bake. Deep-fry at 375°F (190°C) until cooked. Serve with Plum Sauce, page 23, or Mustard Sauce, page 116.

Pictured on page 63.

HAM ROLL

A neat way to fix a ham bite.

Cream cheese	4 oz.	125 g
Mayonnaise	1 tbsp.	15 mL
Worcestershire sauce	1 tsp.	5 mL
Onion salt	¼ tsp.	1 mL
Cooked ham slices	6	6

Mash first 4 ingredients together well.

Spread on ham slices. Roll as for jelly roll. Chill. To serve, cut into slices. Place on plate. These are also suitable to place each slice on a party cracker. Makes 36 or more.

Variation: Add 1 tsp. (5 mL) soy sauce to mixture.

HAM PICKLE ROLL: Fit olives or gherkins across end of cheese-covered ham. Roll. Chill and slice.

MEAT STACKS: Spread 5 slices luncheon meat with cheese mixture. Stack together and cover with sixth slice. Cut into small squares or triangles, or if using round slices, cut into wedges. An olive, pickled onion or gherkin may be speared with a toothpick before spearing each wedge or leave plain. Makes 16.

Pictured on cover.

TOURTIÈRE TARTS

These freeze and reheat beautifully.

Ground beef	1 lb.	500 g
Ground pork	½ lb.	225 g
Small onion, finely chopped	1	1
Salt	¾ tsp.	5 mL
Pepper	¼ tsp.	1 mL
Allspice	¼ tsp.	1 mL
Nutmeg	¼ tsp.	1 mL
Garlic powder	¼ tsp.	1 mL
Water	¾ cup	175 mL
Cooked mashed potato	½ cup	125 mL

Pie crust pastry, your own or a mix

Put first 9 ingredients into large saucepan. Bring to boil. Stir occasionally as it simmers about 15 minutes.

Add mashed potato. Mixture should be moist and thick. Allow to cool completely.

Line tart tins or muffin tins with pastry. Spoon in meat mixture to fill. Moisten edge and cover with small pastry circle cut to fit. Press to seal. Cut 2 or 3 slits in top. Bake in 400°F (200°C) oven until browned.

Variation: This filling may be used to make turnovers and covered rounds also.

Pictured on page 63.

If you roll up your sleeves, chances are that you won't lose your shirt.

Well known and still popular.

Ground beef	1 lb.	500 g
Dry bread crumbs	½ cup	125 mL
Water	½ cup	125 mL
Salt	1 tsp.	5 mL
Pepper	¼ tsp.	1 mL
Cooking oil	2 tbsp.	30 mL
All-purpose flour	4 tbsp.	60 mL
Salt	½ tsp.	2 mL
Pepper	⅛ tsp.	0.5 mL
Milk (or half water)	2 cups	500 mL

Put ground beef, crumbs, water, salt and pepper into bowl. Mix thoroughly. Shape into about 30 balls. Brown in oil in frying pan adding more cooking oil if needed to fry. Remove as cooked. May also be baked in 375°F (190°C) oven for about 15 minutes.

Stir flour into drippings in frying pan. If there is not enough fat to soak up flour, add up to 4 tbsp. (60 mL) butter or margarine. Add salt and pepper. Add milk, stirring to keep from lumping and also to loosen all bits from bottom of pan. A bit of gravy browning may be added if needed for color, but won't be necessary if there are enough brown bits in pan. Add more milk if needed for right consistency. Pour over meatballs in chafing dish. Makes 2½ to 3½ dozen.

SWEET AND SOUR SAUCE

Brown sugar, packed	2 cups	500 mL
All-purpose flour	2 tbsp.	30 mL
Vinegar	½ cup	125 mL
Water	½ cup	125 mL
Soy sauce	2 tbsp.	30 mL
Ketchup	1 tbsp.	15 mL

In saucepan measure brown sugar and flour. Stir well. Add vinegar, water, soy sauce and ketchup. Bring to boil, stirring, over medium heat.

SWEET AND SOUR MEATBALLS: Pour Sweet and Sour Sauce over meatballs in chafing dish.

Pictured on page 63.

GLAZED MEATBALLS

A snap to make. Just put raw meatballs into sauce and cook to a gorgeous glaze.

Ground beef	1½ lbs.	700 g
Dry bread crumbs	¼ cup	50 mL
Water	¼ cup	50 mL
Onion flakes (or ¼ cup, 50 mL, fresh chopped)	2 tsp.	10 mL
Salt	1 tsp.	5 mL
Cinnamon	½ tsp.	2 mL
Pepper	¼ tsp.	1 mL
Grape jelly	1½ cup	375 mL
Ketchup	½ cup	125 mL

Put first 7 ingredients into bowl. Mix well. Shape into small balls.

Heat grape jelly and ketchup in frying pan. Add meatballs. Simmer very slowly for about 20 to 25 minutes turning meatballs at half time. Serve in chafing dish.

Variation: Use crabapple jelly instead of grape. It also gives a great glaze. Makes 36.

SAUCED GARLIC

With crackers and cheese is not the only way to serve this popular sausage. Extra good.

Ketchup	¾ cup	175 mL
Blackberry or grape jelly	¾ cup	175 mL
Prepared mustard	1 tbsp.	15 mL
Soy sauce	1 tsp.	5 mL
Cinnamon	½ tsp.	2 mL
Nutmeg	½ tsp.	2 mL
Ginger	½ tsp.	2 mL
Garlic sausage	1½ lbs.	700 g

Measure first 7 ingredients into saucepan. Heat and stir to dissolve.

Cut sausage into ¼-inch (1 cm) slices. Add to saucepan. Simmer for 10 to 15 minutes. Transfer to chafing dish. Serve with picks. Makes about 4 cups (1 L).

These look dark and even taste dark. Good and a bit different.

Ground beef	1 lb.	500 g
Dry bread crumbs	¼ cup	50 mL
Milk	¼ cup	50 mL
Soy sauce	2 tbsp.	30 mL
Ginger	1 tsp.	5 mL
Rum flavoring	¼ tsp.	1 mL
Garlic powder	¼ tsp.	1 mL

Combine all ingredients in bowl. Mix well. Shape into small balls. Arrange in baking pan. Bake in 375°F (190°C) oven for 10 to 15 minutes. Serve hot with picks and your favorite sauce. Makes 24.

QUICK MEATBALLS: To first 3 ingredients add 1 envelope dry onion soup mix. Shape into small balls. Bake in 375°F (190°C) for about 15 minutes. Serve hot with dipping sauce or in one of the Chafing Dish Sauces page 20.

QUICK OAT MEATBALLS: To ground beef add ¾ cup (175 mL) quick cooking rolled oats, 1 cup (250 mL) tomato juice, 1 egg, beaten, and ½ tsp. (2 mL) dried basil. Shape into small balls. Bake in 375°F (190°C) oven for about 15 minutes. Serve hot with dipping sauce or in one of the Chafing Dish Sauces page 20.

Pictured on page 63.

No wonder the Middle Ages are known as the Dark Ages with so many knights.

POLYNESIAN MEATBALLS

A succulent bite — a hit every time. The sauce makes them perfect.

Ground beef	2 lbs.	1 kg
Soy sauce	3 tbsp.	50 mL
Brown sugar (or granulated)	1 tbsp.	15 mL
Water chestnuts, finely chopped	10 oz.	284 mL
Onion powder	½ tsp.	2 mL
Parsley flakes	1 tsp.	5 mL
Garlic powder (or 2 cloves, minced)	½ tsp.	2 mL

Combine all 7 ingredients in large bowl. Mix well. Shape into 1 inch (2.5 cm) balls. Place on baking sheet with sides. Bake in 375°F (190°C) oven for about 15 minutes. Serve hot with Apricot Sauce. Supply picks. May be reheated in 400°F (200°C) oven for 5 minutes or until hot. Makes about 6½ dozen.

APRICOT SAUCE

Apricot jam	1 cup	250 mL
Cider vinegar	3 tbsp.	50 mL
Paprika	¼ tsp.	1 mL

In small bowl combine jam, vinegar and paprika. Stir well, pour into a pretty bowl and dip in. Just right!

Pictured on page 63.

1. Spiced Nuts page 106
2. Polynesian Nuts page 106
3. Caramel Popcorn page 109
4. Chili Cheese Log page 143
5. Chocolate Nuts page 104
6. Caramelized Almonds with Mixed Nuts page 107
7. Pecan Sandwiches page 108
8. Walnut Sandwiches page 108

You will never go wrong serving this. Positively everyone's favorite.

Thick sirloin steak	1½ lb.	750 g
Soy sauce	¾ cup	175 mL
Packed brown sugar	½ cup	125 mL
Cooking oil	2 tbsp.	30 mL
Garlic powder (or 1 clove, minced)	¼ tsp.	1 mL
Ginger powder	½ tsp.	2 mL

Wooden skewers (soaked in water to prevent scorching)

Slice steak about ⅛ inch (½ cm) thick to make long thin slices. If meat is partially frozen, it is much easier to do.

In bowl, with tight-fitting cover, mix soy sauce, sugar, oil, garlic powder and ginger powder. Put meat into bowl. Press down to cover with marinade. Allow to marinate for at least ½ hour.

Thread meat on skewers accordion-fashion. Broil only until medium-rare. Store, covered in refrigerator. To serve, pile on baking sheet. Heat in 400°F (200°C) oven for about 5 minutes or until hot.

Note: If you have no skewers, slice meat thinly, then into squares. Marinate as above. Transfer meat with slotted spoon to pan with sides. Broil, 1 layer deep, on 1 side only until sizzling and cooked to medium-rare stage. Cool a bit then store in refrigerator. To serve, heat in covered casserole in 350°F (180°C) oven for about 20 minutes or until hot. Serve with picks. Delicious. Serves 12.

Note: Peanut Sauce is often poured over satay before serving. See page 20.

Pictured on cover.

SATAY WITH PINEAPPLE: Thread 2 marinated and broiled meat squares on pick with pineapple chunk in between. Bake as above.

Pictured on page 63.

CHICKEN FINGERS

A good hearty finger food.

Eggs	2	2
Melted butter or cooking oil	1 tbsp.	15 mL
All-purpose flour	1⅓ cups	325 mL
Baking powder	1 tsp.	5 mL
Salt	1 tsp.	5 mL
Pepper	¼ tsp.	1 mL
Water	¾ cup	175 mL
Chicken breasts, boneless	3	3
All-purpose flour		

Fat for deep-frying

Beat eggs until frothy. Stir in butter, first amount of flour, baking powder, salt, pepper and water. Store in covered container in refrigerator to stand for at least 2 hours or up to 10 hours.

Cut chicken into finger-sized pieces. Dredge with flour. Dip in batter. Deep-fry in 375°F (190°C) fat until browned on both sides. Serve with Sweet and Sour Sauce, page 77, Apricot Sauce, page 80, Plum Sauce, page 23, or Barbecue Sauce. Makes about 7 dozen.

Pictured on page 63.

RUMAKI

From Hawaii to you.

Chicken livers, quartered	6	6
Soy sauce	¼ cup	50 mL
Granulated sugar	2 tbsp.	30 mL
Powdered ginger	⅛ tsp.	0.5 mL
Garlic powder	⅛ tsp.	0.5 mL
Water chestnuts, halved	12	12
Bacon slices, cut in half crosswise and half cooked	12	12

(continued on next page)

Put the 24 liver pieces into small bowl. Add soy sauce, sugar, ginger and garlic. Stir well. Let marinate for 1 hour.

Take 1 piece of liver along with 1 water chestnut half and wrap with 1 piece of bacon. Secure with toothpick. Arrange in baking pan. Bake in 450°F (230°C) oven for 10 minutes. Serve hot. Plum Sauce, page 23, and Apricot Sauce, page 80, make good dips. Makes 24.

YAKITORI

These little chicken kabobs are a different but most appealing way to serve a delicious snack. Make plenty.

Soy sauce	¾ cup	175 mL
Granulated sugar	¼ cup	50 mL
Cooking oil	1 tbsp.	15 mL
Garlic powder (or 1 clove, minced)	¼ tsp.	1 mL
Ginger	½ tsp.	2 mL
Chicken breasts, boneless	2	2
Green onions	6 - 8	6 - 8
Wooden skewers or wooden picks (soaked in water to prevent scorching)		

Stir first 5 ingredients together in bowl.

Cut chicken into bite-size pieces. Cut onions into 1-inch (2½ cm) lengths. Put chicken and onion into soy sauce mixture and let marinate for about 30 minutes. Remove with slotted spoon. Thread skewer with 1 chunk of chicken, slide skewer through center of onion section, then add another chicken chunk. Place on rack. Broil about 5 inches from heat, turning and basting with marinade after 3 minutes. Broil another 3 minutes. Makes 20-24.

Note: To serve as an appetizer, allow at least 4 per person, or longer skewer may be used.

SWEET AND SOUR WINGS

Destined to be the highlight of any party.

Chicken wings	3 lbs.	1.5 kg
Salt and pepper, sprinkle		
Brown sugar, packed	1 cup	250 mL
All-purpose flour	¼ cup	50 mL
Water	½ cup	125 mL
Vinegar	¼ cup	50 mL
Soy sauce	¼ cup	50 mL
Ketchup	1 tbsp.	15 mL

Cut off wing tips and discard. Cut wings apart at joint. Place on foil-lined baking sheet with sides. Sprinkle salt and pepper over top. Bake in 350°F (180°C) oven for 30 minutes.

Put sugar and flour into saucepan. Stir thoroughly. Add water, vinegar, soy sauce and ketchup. Stir and cook over medium heat until mixture boils and thickens. Remove from heat. When wings have baked for 30 minutes, brush liberally with sauce. Bake 10 minutes more. Brush with sauce again and bake 10 minutes more. If chicken is tender, remove from oven. If not, brush with sauce once more and continue to bake until done. Serve hot. Makes about 36 pieces.

Pictured on page 63.

If bullets could marry they would have BBs.

These chicken wings marinate as they cook. First rate!

Chicken wings	3 lbs.	1.25 kg
Soy sauce	1 cup	250 mL
Water	½ cup	125 mL
Granulated sugar	½ cup	125 mL
Garlic powder	¼ tsp.	1 mL
Salt	½ tsp.	2 mL
Ginger	¼ tsp.	1 mL

Cut tips from wings and discard. Divide wings at joint into 2 pieces. Place meaty side down in large baking pan such as cake pan or roaster.

Mix next 6 ingredients well. Pour over chicken. Bake uncovered in 325°F (160°) oven for 1½ to 2 hours, depending on size of wings, until tender. Turn chicken pieces after ¾ hour. Remove with tongs to serving platter. Makes about 36 pieces.

PARMESAN CHICKEN WINGS

You will have everyone exclaiming over these. Better make lots.

Grated Parmesan cheese	1 cup	250 mL
Parsley flakes	1 tsp.	5 mL
Paprika	1 tsp.	5 mL
Salt	1 tsp.	5 mL
Pepper	¼ tsp.	1 mL
Garlic powder	¼ tsp.	1 mL
Chicken wings	2 lbs.	1 kg
Butter or margarine	½ cup	125 mL

Measure first 6 ingredients into bowl. Mix well.

Cut off wing tips and discard. Separate wings at joint. Dip each piece in melted butter, then in cheese mixture. Coat completely. Place on foil-lined baking sheet with sides. Bake uncovered in 350°F (180°C) oven for about 45 minutes until tender. Serve hot. Makes about 24 pieces.

Note: Adding a few fine bread crumbs to the cheese mixture makes it go further. Too many will weaken the flavor.

Pictured on page 63.

CORNISH PASTIES

The filling is cooked ahead for both ease and speed in preparation. A small version of a miner's lunch.

Butter or margarine	2 tbsp.	30 mL
Medium onion, chopped	1	1
Ground beef (or finely diced sirloin steak)	¾ lb.	375 g
Medium-large potato, diced	1	1
Diced turnip (optional but good)	½ cup	125 mL
Salt	1 tsp.	5 mL
Pepper	¼ tsp.	1 mL
Pie crust pastry, your own or a mix		
Egg, beaten	1	1

Melt butter in frying pan. Add onions and sauté for 2 or 3 minutes. Add ground beef. Scramble-fry until browned.

Add potato, turnip, salt and pepper. Cook, stirring frequently, for about 4 or 5 minutes. Allow to cool.

Roll pastry and cut into 3 or 4-inch (7 or 10 cm) circles. Place small spoonful in center. Dampen outer edge of circle. Gather edges to top so as to form seam in the center. Press to seal, or fold over and seal. Arrange on baking sheet. Prick holes on top.

Brush with egg. Bake in 400°F (200°C) oven for about 20 minutes until browned well. Makes 6-7 dozen.

No stranger to religion, each skunk has its own pew.

An all-time winner. More garlic can easily be added if you would like a stronger flavor.

Spare ribs, bones cut in short lengths	**2 lbs.**	**1 kg**
Soy sauce	**2 tbsp.**	**30 mL**
Water	**2 tbsp.**	**30 mL**
Brown sugar	**1 tbsp.**	**15 mL**
Garlic powder	**1 tsp.**	**5 mL**
Salt	**½ tsp.**	**2 mL**
Ginger	**¼ tsp.**	**1 mL**
All-purpose flour	**¼ cup**	**50 mL**
Eggs, slightly beaten	**4**	**4**

Fat for deep-frying

Cut meat between bones. Set aside.

Measure soy sauce, water, sugar, garlic powder, salt and ginger into large bowl. Stir in flour. Add eggs and mix. Add ribs and stir carefully into mixture. Let stand ½ hour.

Deep-fry a few at a time in hot fat 375°F (190°C) until browned.

QUICK DRY RIBS: To 1 package (2 envelopes) of Regular Chicken Shake and Bake, add 1 tsp. (5 mL) garlic powder and put into bag. Shake damp ribs, a few at a time, to coat. Deep-fry. These ribs will not have as much batter on them. They are delicious. Serves 6.

Pirate days aren't over. There are still lots around who know how to rig a sale.

WIENER BITES

These are among the best. You will have to make this in multiple quantities. Freezes well.

Wieners, cut in 6 pieces	8	8
Wide bacon slices (or twice the number of narrow slices)	12	12

Wieners that are 5 inches (13 cm) in length can be cut into 6 pieces each for bite-size servings.

Fry bacon slices until fat part has lost its whiteness. Do not fry until crisp or it won't roll. Cut slice in half crosswise and lengthwise. When cool enough to handle, wrap around wiener section and secure with toothpick. Uncooked bacon may be used but it takes longer to cook (they need broiling) at the last minute.

To serve: Arrange on baking tray (or plate for microwave) and heat in hot oven 400°F (200°C) until sizzling hot. Can be kept hot on hot serving tray. Makes 48.

Pictured on page 63.

WEE FRANKS

Any age group will devour these in no time.

Ketchup	½ cup	125 mL
Currant jelly, red or black or blackberry jelly	½ cup	125 mL
Dry onion flakes	1 tsp.	5 mL
Wieners, cut bite-size	1 lb.	450 g

Measure ketchup, jelly and onion into saucepan. Stir.

Add wieners. Bring to boil. Allow to simmer slowly, covered, 30-45 minutes. Transfer to chafing dish. Supply picks. Makes 72.

Chilee-cahn-KAY-soh is a mild cream cheese dip served warm with tortilla chips. Just as delicious with potato chips. Excellent.

Velveeta cheese	1 lb.	500 g
Light cream	¾ cup	175 mL
Can of chopped green chilies	4 oz.	114 g
Finely chopped green pepper	¼ cup	50 mL
Chopped pimiento	4 tsp.	20 mL

Cut Velveeta cheese into chunks into a heavy saucepan or top of a double boiler. Add cream and chopped chilies. Cook green pepper 2 minutes on high power in microwave or boil until tender-crisp. Add to cheese mixture along with pimiento. Melt together stirring frequently. Heat slowly. If heated too fast or too hot, cheese may go stringy. Serve warm with tortilla chips. Your own are best. Better to make a day ahead so flavors blend. Makes about 3 cups (700 mL).

CHILI CON QUESO SAUCE: Pour over enchiladas, burros, and any other food that a good sauce enhances.

Note: If Velveeta is not available, use another mild, soft, processed cheese.

Note: To thicken, mix 1 tbsp (15 mL) water with 1 tbsp. (15 mL) cornstarch and add to hot sauce, stir until bubbly hot.

Pictured on page 99.

GUACAMOLE DIP

A touch of Mexico.

Ripe avocados, peeled and mashed	2	2
Lemon juice	2 tbsp.	30mL
Onion flakes	2 tsp.	10 mL
Salt	1 tsp.	5 mL
Pepper	¼ tsp.	1 mL
Cayenne pepper	¼ tsp.	1 mL
Garlic powder	¼ tsp.	1 mL
Ripe tomato, diced	1	1

Mix all ingredients together. Serve with corn chips, tortilla chips or fresh raw vegetables. If you would like to add garnish, parsley is a good choice. Makes about 1 cup (250 mL).

TOSTADOS

A toe-STAH-dah is a Mexican open-faced sandwich. Make tiny for hors d'oeuvres and regular for first-course appetizers.

Tortillas	6	6
Cooking oil		
Refried beans (or ground beef, fried)	1 cup	250 mL
Salsa	6 tbsp.	100 mL
Shredded Monterey Jack cheese	1 cup	250 mL
Shredded lettuce	2 cups	500 mL
Shredded Cheddar cheese	½ cup	125 mL
Chopped green onions	2 tbsp.	30 mL

Fry tortillas in hot oil in frying pan until crisp.

Divide remaining ingredients, in order given, among the 6 tortillas. Serves 6 as a sit-down appetizer or more if smaller tortillas are used.

Note: Instead of using refried beans or ground beef, both may be used if your prefer.

TOSTADO HORS D'OEUVRES: Use round tortilla chips. You now have tostaditos. Make only ¼ or ½ recipe of topping.

Pictured on page 99.

CORN CHIPS

Tor-TEE-yahs can be put to good use this way. You get the best when you make your own chips.

Package of tortillas	1	1
Fat for deep-frying		

Cut each tortilla into 8 pie-shaped wedges. Deep-fry in hot fat 375°F (190°C) until crisp. Drain on paper towels. Serve with Chili Con Queso, page 91, Salsa, page 94, Guacamole, page 91, or any other dip. Serves 6.

Note: For fat-free chips, bake in 425°F (220°C) oven for about 8 minutes until golden and crisp.

Pictured on page 99.

NAH-chohs are corn chips served with melted cheese on them. They can be more elaborate with several additions. Cheese strips may be used rather than shredded cheese. They don't topple off the chips.

Corn chips		
Shredded mild Cheddar cheese, Monterey Jack or cheese spread	**1 cup**	**250 mL**
Bacon slices, cooked and crumbled or bacon bits	**4**	**4**
Green onions, chopped	**4**	**4**

Crowd chips on baking sheet. Put about 1 tbsp. (15 mL) cheese on each. Add some bacon pieces and top with green onions. Bake in 350°F (180°C) oven for 10 minutes or until hot and cheese is melted. May be served with sour cream or Salsa, page 94, for dipping. Make 1½ - 2 dozen.

Note: To make the quickest and best nachos, microwave ½ cup (125 mL) cheese spread (such as Cheese Whiz) on medium power for 2 minutes, or heat in saucepan. Pour over crowded nachos. Serve with sour cream for dipping.

NACHO VARIATIONS
1. Grated cheese, salsa, green onions
2. Grated cheese, sliced olive, pepperoni slice
3. Refried beans, grated cheese, dab of sour cream
4. Tomato paste, grated Cheddar, jalapeño slice
5. Salsa, grated Cheddar
6. Grated Cheddar, jalapeño slice
7. Chili con carne, grated cheese
8. Refried beans, grated cheese, jalapeño slice

Pictured on page 99.

SALSA

You will find this type of sauce always on a Mexican table. A hot sauce, it can be made as hot as you like.

Canned tomatoes	2-14 oz.	2-398 mL
Green pepper, cut in pieces	1	1
Chopped onion	½ cup	125 mL
Garlic powder (or 1 clove, minced)	¼ tsp.	1 mL
Salt	¼ tsp.	1 mL
Canned pickled jalapeño pepper slices (or more)	4	4

Put all ingredients into blender. Blend smooth. Pour into saucepan. Bring to boil. Simmer slowly for 10 minutes. Cool and pour into container. Serve as a sauce or a dip for corn chips. Makes 3 cups (675 mL).

Pictured on page 99.

SALSA CRUDA

SAHL-sah CROO-dah is a red sauce found on Mexican tables. This is a milder uncooked sauce.

Tomatoes, diced	2	2
Minced onion	½ cup	125 mL
Green onions, chopped	2	2
Cooking oil	1 tbsp.	15 mL
Granulated sugar	1 tsp.	5 mL
Salt	½ tsp.	2 mL
Canned chopped green chilies, drained and chopped more yet	4 oz.	114 g

Combine all ingredients. Chill for at least 2 hours before using. Use as a sauce or serve with corn chips. Makes 2½ cups (570 mL).

Pictured on page 99.

These beef turnovers were the inspiration of someone in Argentina. Delicious in regular or cheese pastry.

CHEESE PASTRY

Cream cheese, room temperature	8 oz.	250 g
Butter or margarine, softened	½ cup	125 mL
All purpose flour	1½ cups	375 mL

Beat cheese and butter together. Mix in flour. Form into ball. chill 1 hour.

FILLING

Cooking oil	1 tbsp.	15 mL
Onion, minced	3 tbsp.	50 mL
Ground beef	½ lb.	250 g
Canned tomatoes, drained and mashed	½ cup	125 mL
Raisins, chopped	2 tbsp.	30 mL
Green olives, chopped	2 tbsp.	30 mL
Worcestershire sauce	1 tbsp.	15 mL
Salt	½ tsp.	2 mL
Oregano (optional)	½ tsp.	2 mL
Hard-boiled egg, chopped	1	1
Egg, slightly beaten	1	1
Sesame seeds	¼ cup	50 mL

Combine oil, onion and beef in frying pan. Scramble-fry until browned. Stir in next 6 ingredients. Simmer for 5 minutes, stirring frequently. Cool.

Stir in chopped egg.

Roll pastry fairly thin on a lightly floured surface. Cut into 3-inch (7½ cm) rounds. Put 1 tsp. (5 mL) in center of each. Moisten half of outside edge with egg. Fold over to seal. Press with fork tines. Transfer to ungreased baking sheet.

Cut small slits in top. Brush with egg. Sprinkle with sesame seeds. Bake in 400°F (200°C) oven for 12 - 15 minutes until browned. Serve hot. Makes 3½ - 4 dozen.

Pictured on page 99.

CHIMICHANGAS

Chim-mee-CHAN-gas are burritos that are deep-fried. Soft flour tortillas are used to make these.

Lard or cooking oil	2 tbsp.	30 mL
Beef stew meat, cut in small cubes	1 lb.	500 g
Boiling water	1 cup	250 mL
Beef bouillon cubes	2	2
Medium onion, chopped	1	1
Butter or margarine	2 tbsp.	30 mL
Salt	1 tsp.	5 mL
Garlic powder (or 1 clove, minced)	¼ tsp.	1 mL
Tomato, cut up	1	1
Canned chopped green chilies, drained, no seeds	4 oz.	114 g
Flour tortillas (soft)	6	6
Fat for deep-frying		
Shredded Cheddar or Monterey Jack cheese for topping		
Red salsa or taco sauce, warmed a bit		

Heat fat in roaster. Add meat and brown well over medium heat. Measure water. Stir in beef cubes. Stir to dissolve. Pour over meat.

Put next 6 ingredients into blender. Blend together. Pour over meat. Stir. Cover. Bake in 300°F (150°C) oven for 2 hours until meat is very tender. If pieces are large, shred with fork. If there is a lot of sauce, boil on stove, uncovered, to evaporate most of it.

Spoon ⅙ of the meat mixture along side of a tortilla. Turn side over, fold ends in and roll up. Pin with toothpick to keep filling in. Deep-fry seam side down and turn to brown both sides. Drain on paper towels.

Sprinkle with cheese. Spoon sauce over top. Serves 6 as a sit-down appetizer.

For small finger food, cut flour tortillas or soften corn tortillas and roll. Omit sauce over top. Use as a dip instead.

(continued on next page)

BURRITOS: Bur-EE-tohs: Instead of deep-frying, place rolled tortillas in baking pan. Cover with foil. Bake in 350°F (180°C) oven for 15 minutes or until hot. Put on 6 plates and spoon warm Chili Con Queso, page 91, over each. Makes 6 appetizers.

Pictured on page 99.

JALAPEÑO JELLY

Hahl-ah-PAIN-yoh jelly is different and a treat to eat.

Canned chopped pickled jalapeño peppers (or more)	¼ cup	50 mL
Chopped red pepper	¾ cup	175 mL
Vinegar	1 cup	250 mL
Lemon juice	3 tbsp.	50 mL
Granulated sugar	5 cups	1.25 L
Bottle of Certo, 6 oz. (170 mL) size	½ btl.	½ btl.

Put jalapeño and red pepper into blender. Add half of the vinegar. Blend smooth. Pour into large saucepan. Add rest of vinegar, lemon juice and sugar. Bring to boil, stirring often. Boil for 10 minutes. Add Certo. Return to full rolling boil. Boil 1 minute. Remove from heat and skim. Pour into sterilized jars. Seal with melted paraffin. Makes 4 jars, 8 oz. (225 mL) size. Spread crackers with cream cheese and top with jelly.

JALAPEÑO CHEESE: Place cream cheese on shallow plate. Cover with jalapeño jelly. Serve with assorted crackers.

Pictured on page 99.

The rabbits in Paris are raised in the hutch back of Notre Dame.

CHICKEN NACHOS

NAH-chos are so popular with so many varieties. You will enjoy these as a sit-down appetizer or as finger food.

Tortilla shells	6	6
Cooked chicken, shredded	1½ cup	375 mL
Salsa	6 tbsp.	90 mL
Ripe olives, sliced	6	6
Green onions, chopped	6	6
Sour cream	¾ cup	175 mL
Monterey Jack cheese (or mozzarella)	1½ cups	375 mL
Canned jalapeño pickled pepper slices	24	24

Place tortilla shells on baking sheet.

Divide chicken among tortillas. Leave 1 inch (2½ cm) all around the outside free of chicken. Put 1 tbsp. (15 mL) Salsa, page 94, on top. Sprinkle with olives followed by onions.

Put 2 tbsp. (30 mL) sour cream on each, then ¼ cup (50 mL) shredded Monterey Jack cheese. Bake in 400°F (200°C) oven for 20 minutes until hot and cheese is melted. Cut into quarters to serve. Top each quarter with jalapeño slice. Place 4 quarters, reshaped into circle, as a sit-down appetizer or serve as finger food. Makes 6 appetizers or 24 hors d'oeuvres.

1. Jalapeño Jelly page 97
2. Nachos page 93
3. Chilies Rellenos Squares page 103
4. Chimichangas page 96
5. Burritos page 97
6. Chili Con Queso page 91
7. Salsa page 94
8. Salsa Cruda page 94
9. Corn Chips page 92
10. Empanadas page 95
11. Tostado Hors d'oeuvres, Tostaditos page 92

These cheese crisps, kay-sah-DEE-yahs, may be served as a sit-down appetizer or cut into smaller sections for finger hors d'oeuvres.

Flour tortillas	4	4
Shredded Cheddar or Monterey Jack cheese	½ cup	125 mL
Chopped green chilies, no seeds	4 oz.	114 g
Tomato, diced	1	1
Green onions, chopped	2	2

Cooking oil or lard

Lay tortilla on working surface. Dip your hand in water, pat tortilla lightly, repeating until the top side is quite moist. Place 2 tbsp. (30 mL) cheese on top which would be ¼ of the total amount. Put ¼ green chilies, ¼ tomato and ¼ onions over top of cheese. Fold tortilla over and fasten with a toothpick as though you were pinning it closed with a straight pin.

Fry in hot fat at least ½ inch (1 cm) deep. Turn often. Press edges together as it fries. Brown both sides. Repeat with other 3 tortillas. Serve hot. May be topped with Guacamole Sauce, page 91. Makes 4 appetizers.

Variation: Bake in 350°F (180°C) oven for 10 to 15 minutes until cheese is melted. Cut in pie-shaped wedges to serve. Great finger food.

Actually, Adam paid less attention to the apple on the tree than to the tomato on the ground.

CHILIES RELLENOS

A chili ree-AY-noh is a pepper stuffed with cheese and then deep-fried in a very different egg batter. Listed are two methods of deep-frying.

Canned green chilies (whole)	2 × 4 oz.	2 × 114 g
Monterey Jack cheese strips	6	6
Egg whites	6	6
Egg yolks	6	6
All-purpose flour	½ cup	125 mL
All-purpose flour for dipping		
Fat for deep-frying		

Cut slit in chilies. Insert a strip of cheese carefully in each.

Beat egg whites until stiff. Fold in egg yolks and flour.

Dip stuffed chili into flour to coat, then dip into egg batter. Lower into fat to deep-fry. Cook about 2 or 3 minutes per side until browned. Remove. Serve hot with Quick Tomato Sauce. Makes 6 appetizers.

Variation: In frying pan containing at least ½ inch (1 cm) hot fat, use 2 spoons to shape some batter to a bit larger size than stuffed chili. Place chili on batter. Cover with more batter sealing edges all around. Fry for 2 or 3 minutes then turn carefully using spoons so as not to splash fat. Brown both sides. Serve hot with Quick Tomato Sauce.

QUICK TOMATO SAUCE

Boiling water	1 cup	250 mL
Beef bouillon cube	1	1
Butter or margarine	3 tbsp.	50 mL
All-purpose flour	3 tbsp.	50 mL
Tomato sauce	1 cup	250 mL

Measure water. Add bouillon cube and stir to dissolve. Set aside.

Melt butter in saucepan. Mix in flour. Add tomato sauce and beef bouillon. Stir and bring to boil to thicken. Spoon over Chilies Rellenos and serve. Makes 2 cups (500 mL)

CHILIES RELLENOS SQUARES

Just cut this pan of Chilies ree-AY-nohs into squares and serve.

Canned green chilies (whole)	2 × 4 oz.	2 × 114 g
Monterey Jack cheese, grated	1 lb.	455 g
Eggs	2	2
Sour cream	1 cup	250 mL
Salt	¼ tsp.	1 mL
Pepper	⅛ tsp.	0.5 mL

Remove seeds from chilies. Cut pieces flat. Put 1 layer in greased 8x8-inch (20x20 cm) pan. Sprinkle with ½ of the cheese. Spread rest of chilies then the rest of the cheese.

Beat eggs until frothy. Add sour cream, salt and pepper. Mix. Pour over chili layers. Bake uncovered in 350°F (180°C) oven for 45 minutes, until set. Serve hot. Serves 9. Also may be cut into 1-inch (2½ cm) squares. Makes 64 hors d'oeuvres.

Pictured on page 99.

ENCHILADAS

An ahn-che-LAH-dah is a tortilla, stuffed with a spicy sauce.

Butter or margarine	2 tbsp.	30 mL
Large onion, chopped	1	1
Tortillas	6	6
Oil		
Chili sauce	1 cup	250 mL
Shredded Monterey Jack cheese	2 cups	500 mL
Shredded Cheddar cheese	1 cup	250 mL

Put butter and onions in frying pan. Sauté until clear and soft.

Dip tortillas in hot oil in pan to soften. Dip in chili sauce.

Divide ½ Monterey Jack, ½ Cheddar and ½ onion among tortillas. Roll and place close together in pan. Pour remaining chili sauce over. Sprinkle cheese and onion over top. Bake covered in 350°F (180°C) oven for 20 minutes. Serves 6.

HAMBURGER ENCHILADA: Add from ½ to 1 pound (250-500 g) ground beef to the onions when frying.

ALMOND SPECIAL

Such a fresh flavor! It's hard to get enough of these.

Natural almonds (with brown skin on) or other natural nuts	1½ cups	200 g
Butter or margarine	1 tbsp.	15 mL
Salt	¼ tsp.	1 mL

Put almonds and butter into frying pan. Fry, stirring often, for about 5 to 10 minutes until browned. Sprinkle with salt, toss to coat. Cool. Makes 1½ cups (350 mL).

BARBECUED PEANUTS

This makes a welcome change from the ordinary. So easy.

Peanuts	2 cups	500 mL
Barbecue sauce, plain	4 tsp.	25 mL
Paprika	¼ tsp.	1 mL
Cayenne pepper	⅛ tsp.	0.5 mL

Combine all ingredients in bowl. Stir until peanuts are well coated. Spread in large ungreased baking pan. Bake in 300°F (150°C) oven for about 20 minutes. Stir at half time. Peanuts should be fairly dry. Cool. Store in airtight container. Makes 2 cups (500 mL).

CHOCOLATE NUTS

Ready in a jiffy. Different and good, a hint of chocolate.

Pecan or walnut halves	1 cup	250 mL
Warm water to cover		
Chocolate drink powder	2 tbsp.	30 mL

Put nuts and warm water into small bowl. Let soak for 10 minutes.

Drain nuts and combine with chocolate drink powder. Stir well until all nuts are thoroughly coated. Spread in large greased baking pan. Heat in 350°F (180°C) oven for 5 minutes or so until showing signs of drying and crisping. Makes 1 cup (250 mL).

Pictured on page 81.

One of the best. Quick to disappear. Freezes well.

Cheerios, box	1	1
Shreddies, box	1	1
Pretzels, box (break in half)	½	½
Large peanuts	2 cups	500 mL
Butter or margarine	1 cup	250 mL
Seasoned salt	2 tbsp.	30 mL
Onion powder	1 tbsp.	15 mL
Garlic powder	1 tsp.	5 mL

Put first 4 ingredients into large roaster.

Melt butter in small saucepan. Stir in seasoned salt, onion powder and garlic powder. Drizzle over contents in roaster. Stir carefully to mix together well. Roast uncovered in 250°F (120°C) oven for 1½ hours. Stir about every 20 minutes while roasting. Cool. Store in airtight containers. Makes 5 quarts. (6 L).

Variation: Use mixed nuts if desired. Keeping proportions in mind, substitute another type of cereal if you would rather.

Note: A box of Cheerios contains about 12 cups (3 L). A box of Shreddies contains about 13 cups (3 L). A box of pretzels broken in half contains about 4-5 cups (1 L). Knowing this enables you to make up a smaller portion if desired. For about 6 cups (1.4 L) cereal, which would be ¼ of the recipe, 45 minutes roasting time is adequate.

A good magician is a super duper.

POLYNESIAN NUTS

The host with the most or the hostess with the mostest - that's what you'll be when you have these on hand.

Butter or margarine, melted	2 tbsp.	30 mL
Macadamia nuts, almonds or pecans	2 cups	500 mL
Soy sauce	2 tsp.	10 mL
Salt	½ tsp.	2 mL
Cayenne pepper	⅛ tsp.	0.5 mL

Put melted butter and nuts into small bowl. Stir until nuts are coated. Transfer to baking sheet. Toast in 325°F (150°C) oven for about 15 to 20 minutes stirring twice. Remove from oven.

Sprinkle soy sauce, salt and cayenne over top. Stir well to distribute evenly. Cool before storing in an airtight container. Makes 2 cups (500 mL).

Pictured on page 81.

SPICED NUTS

An extra special appetizer. You will need more than one dishful. Makes a good gift.

Egg white, slightly beaten	1	1
Mixed nuts	2 cups	500 mL
Granulated sugar	6 tbsp.	100 mL
Cinnamon	1 tbsp.	15 mL
Nutmeg	⅛ tsp.	0.5 mL
Cloves	⅛ tsp.	0.5 mL
Raisins	1 cup	250 mL
Salt	½ tsp.	2 mL

Beat egg white until smooth consistency. Add nuts. Stir to coat each nut.

Mix sugar, cinnamon, nutmeg and cloves together in small container. Stir into nut mixture. Spread on baking sheet. Bake in 325°F (160°C) oven for about 20 minutes stirring 2 or 3 times.

Remove from oven, stir in raisins and salt right away. Allow to cool. Store in covered container. Makes 3 cups (750 mL).

(continued on next page)

Note: Slivered almonds, pecan halves, walnut halves or peanuts may be used in place of mixed nuts. Adding a few candied cherries makes it super special.

Pictured on page 81.

CARAMELIZED ALMONDS

Very versatile. Equally good using almonds with or without skins. Add a few pecans or walnuts or use mixed nuts. Good.

Shelled whole almonds	2 cups	500 mL
Granulated sugar	1 cup	250 mL
Water	½ cup	125 mL
Salt	½ tsp.	2 mL

Combine all ingredients in heavy saucepan. Cook and stir over medium heat until a light caramel color. Spread on greased cookie sheet. Using 2 forks, separate nuts or cool first then break apart. Store in airtight container in cool place. Makes 2 cups (500 mL).

ORANGE ALMONDS: Add grated rind of 1 orange to ingredients in saucepan. Added zip!

CARAMELIZED PEANUTS: Omit almonds, using peanuts instead. It makes a more economical treat.

CANDIED CINNAMON NUTS: Using whatever nuts you prefer, add ½ tsp. (2 mL) cinnamon and 1 tsp. (5 mL) vanilla.

Pictured on page 81.

If girls whistle at you as you go by, would they be tweet walkers?

TRAIL MIX

A winning mixture, extra good snacking.

Butter or margarine	2 tbsp.	30 mL
Broken cashews	1 cup	250 mL
Peanuts	1 cup	250 mL
Sunflower seeds	½ cup	125 mL
Dried apricots, cut in quarters	1 cup	250 mL
Light raisins	1 cup	250 mL
Dark raisins	1 cup	250 mL
Currants	½ cup	125 mL
Salt sprinkle		

Put butter, cashews, peanuts and sunflower seeds into frying pan. Heat, stirring frequently, until toasty brown. Cool.

Add apricots, raisins and currants. Stir. Sprinkle with a bit of salt to taste. Makes 6 cups (1.5 L).

NATURAL TRAIL MIX: Omit butter and salt. Combine rest of ingredients together. A few chopped dates may be added along with almonds. Pretty it up with candied cherries. Store covered. Makes about 6 cups (1.5 L).

WALNUT SANDWICHES

These little sandwiched nuts make a too-hard-to-resist bite.

Cream cheese, softened	4 tbsp.	50 mL
Onion salt	⅛ tsp.	0.5 mL
Paprika	⅛ tsp.	0.5 mL
Walnut halves		

Mash cream cheese with onion salt and paprika.

Spread walnut halves with some cheese mixture. Press with more halves to make "sandwiches". Makes about 18.

PECAN SANDWICHES: Use pecans in place of walnuts. Makes a bit smaller nibble.

Pictured on page 81.

This won't last long at snack time. Great for lunch bags. It freezes well too. Good for birthday parties.

Popcorn (pop about 1 cup, 250 mL)	5-6 qts.	6-7 L
Butter or margarine	1 cup	250 mL
Brown sugar, packed	2 cups	500 mL
Corn syrup	½ cup	125 mL
Salt	1 tsp.	5 mL
Vanilla	1 tsp.	5 mL
Baking soda	½ tsp.	3 mL

Have popcorn ready in extra-large container.

Combine butter, brown sugar, syrup and salt in heavy saucepan. Heat and stir over medium heat until boiling. Boil without stirring for 5 minutes.

Stir in vanilla and baking soda. Pour over popcorn. Toss together well until all pieces are coated. Spread on 2 large ungreased shallow pans. Bake in 250°F (135°C) oven for 1 hour, stirring every 15 minutes. Cool thoroughly. Break apart and pack in plastic bags.

Variation: Add up to 2 cups (500 mL) peanuts to smaller quantity of popcorn in container before adding syrup mixture.

SPECIAL CARAMEL CORN. Use only 4 qts. (5 L) popcorn or 1½ times the quantity of syrup for 6 qts. (7 L) of popcorn and 2 cups (500 mL) peanuts. Extra delicious.

Pictured on page 81.

Rivers become crooked by following the line of least resistance. So do some people.

BABY CHEDDAR TARTS

These cute little duffers are every bit as good as they look.

PASTRY

Butter or margarine, softened	½ cup	125 mL
Cream cheese, softened	4 oz.	125 g
All-purpose flour	1 cup	250 mL

Beat butter and cream cheese until smooth and light. Work in flour. Roll into long thin roll. Mark off, then cut into 24 pieces. Press into small tart tins to form shells.

FILLING

Grated Cheddar cheese	1 cup	250 mL
Egg	1	1
Milk	½ cup	125 mL
Salt	¼ tsp.	1 mL
Onion salt	¼ tsp.	1 mL

Divide cheese evenly among tart shells.

Beat egg until frothy. Mix in milk, salt and onion salt. Spoon into shells. Bake in 350°F (180°C) oven for about 20 to 25 minutes until set. Makes 24.

BABY SWISS TARTS: Use grated Swiss cheese instead of Cheddar. May be baked in pie plate to be used as an appetizer.

CRAB TARTLETS

Dainty to look at, delectable to eat.

Unbaked pastry-lined small tart tins	60	60
Eggs	2	2
All-purpose flour	2 tbsp.	30 mL
Mayonnaise	½ cup	125 mL
Milk	½ cup	125 mL
Green onions, finely chopped	3	3
Crabmeat	4¾ oz.	135 g
Grated Swiss cheese	2 cups	500 mL

(continued on next page)

Prepare pastry shells.

Beat eggs until frothy. Mix in flour, mayonnaise and milk. Add onion. Remove membranes from crab. Stir in crab and cheese. Pour into shells. Bake on lowest rack in 350°F (180°C) oven for 30 minutes or until set. Makes 5 dozen 1½-inch (4 cm) tarts.

CRAB QUICHE: Pour into unbaked 9-inch (23 cm) pie shell. Bake about 40 minutes until set. Serves 8 to 10 as a first course appetizer.

ONION QUICHE

Everyone loves onion-flavored food. This is onion at its best. Has the appearance of custard pudding.

Unbaked 9-inch (23 cm) pie shell	1	1
Large onions, chopped	2	2
Butter or margarine	3 tbsp.	50 mL
Eggs	3	3
Sour cream	1 cup	250 mL
Milk	¼ cup	50 mL
Salt	1 tsp.	5 mL
Pepper	¼ tsp.	1 mL
Grated Parmesan cheese	½ cup	125 mL
Paprika		

Have pie shell ready.

Sauté onions in butter until soft and clear.

Beat eggs until frothy. Add sour cream, milk, salt and pepper. Beat to mix. Add onions. Stir. Pour into pie shell.

Scatter cheese over top. Sprinkle with paprika. Bake on lowest shelf in 350°F (180°C) oven for about 30 minutes. Test by inserting a knife close to the center. It should come out clean. Serve immediately. Makes 8 to 10 appetizers.

ONION TARTS: This may be made into small individual tarts or in 4-inch (10 cm) pie plates to be cut into quarters.

COCKTAIL QUICHE LORRAINE

Thanks to Alsace Lorraine, this first quiche is still a favorite.

Unbaked small pastry tart shells Use cheese pastry or regular pie pastry.	48	48

FILLING

Bacon slices, cooked and crumbled	8	8
Shredded Swiss cheese (or half Swiss and half Cheddar)	1 cup	250 mL
Eggs	3	3
Cream or rich milk	1½ cups	375 mL
Dry onion flakes	2 tsp.	10 mL
Salt	½ tsp.	2 mL
Pepper	¼ tsp.	1 mL
Nutmeg	⅛ tsp.	0.5 mL

Prepare tart shells.

Divide bacon and cheese among tart shells.

Beat eggs until frothy. Stir in cream, onion flakes, salt, pepper and nutmeg. Pour over bacon-cheese mixture. Bake in 350°F (180°C) oven for about 30 minutes or until set. Nicer served hot. Makes 4 dozen 1½-inch (4 cm) tarts.

QUICHE LORRAINE: Pour filling into unbaked 9-inch (23 cm) pie shell. Bake in 350°F (180°C) oven for about 45 minutes until knife inserted near center comes out clean. Cut into wedges to serve. Nicer served hot. Makes 8 to 10 first course appetizers.

If you see an Indian hitch-hiking in October, you have seen a real Indian thumber.

The pizza flavor is quite mild. Good.

Pastry for a 10-inch (25 cm) pie crust, your own or a mix.

Shredded mozzarella cheese	⅓ cup	75 mL
Shredded Cheddar cheese	⅓ cup	75 mL
Grated Romano or Parmesan cheese	⅓ cup	75 mL
Green onions, finely chopped	2-3	2-3
Eggs	3	3
Milk	1 cup	250 mL
Salt	½ tsp.	2 mL
Pepper	¼ tsp.	1 mL
Oregano	¼ tsp.	1 mL
Garlic powder	¼ tsp.	1 mL
Small ripe tomatoes, thinly sliced	2	2
Grated Parmesan cheese	⅓ cup	75 mL

Roll pastry to fit pie plate.

Sprinkle next 4 ingredients over pie shell in order given.

Beat eggs until frothy. Add milk, salt, pepper, oregano and garlic powder. Beat to mix. Pour over cheese-onion layers in pie shell.

Arrange tomato slices over top. Sprinkle with Parmesan cheese. Bake in 350°F (180°C) oven for about 25 minutes until firm. Serve warm, cut into wedges. Serves 10 as a pre-dinner appetizer or 6 as an evening snack.

OLIVE QUICHE: Sprinkle ⅓ cup (75 mL) sliced stuffed green olives over cheese-onion mixture before pouring egg mixture over top.

Little Tommy had to quit tap-dancing. He kept falling in the sink.

HURRIED ONION QUICHE

This quickie tastes like French onion soup.

Unbaked 9-inch (23 cm) pie shell	1	1
Eggs	3	3
Envelope dry onion soup mix	1½ oz.	42.5 g
Milk	1¼ cups	300 mL
Salt (optional)	¼ tsp.	1 mL
Dry mustard powder	¼ tsp.	1 mL
Cayenne pepper	¼ tsp.	1 mL
Pepper	⅛ tsp.	0.5 mL
Swiss cheese, grated	2 cups	500 mL

Beat eggs until frothy. Add onion soup mix. Beat until mixed. Stir in milk, salt, mustard, cayenne and pepper. Add cheese. Mix and pour into pie shell. Bake on lowest shelf in 350°F (180°C) oven for about 30 minutes until a knife inserted near the center comes out clean. Serve hot. Makes 8 to 10 appetizers.

HURRIED ONION TARTS: This recipe makes 2½ cups (625 mL) of filling which is sufficient for 12 large 2½-inch (6½ cm) tart shells as well as 2 small 6-inch (15 cm) foil pie plates.

SHRIMP QUICHE

A real treat for either expected or unexpected company. A good freezer delicacy. Great evening snack as well as pre-dinner.

Pastry, your own or a mix

Tin of small broken shrimp	4 oz.	113 g
Finely chopped onion	¼ cup	50 mL
Shredded Swiss cheese	1 cup	250 mL
Eggs	2	2
Mayonnaise	½ cup	125 mL
Milk	⅓ cup	75 mL
Salt	¼ tsp	1 mL
Dried dill weed	¼ tsp.	1 mL

Line 12 muffin cups with pastry. Set aside.

Rinse and drain shrimp and divide equally among pastry shells. Divide onion next followed by the Swiss cheese.

(continued on next page)

Beat eggs until frothy. Add mayonnaise, milk, salt and dill weed. Beat to mix. Pour over top of shrimp mixture in shells. Bake in 400°F (200°C) oven for 15-20 minutes until nicely browned. Serve warm. Makes 12.

REUBEN QUICHE

What a different, delicious way to enjoy a popular combination! No eggs.

BOTTOM CRUST

All-purpose flour	2 cups	500 mL
Granulated sugar	2 tbsp.	30 mL
Baking powder	4 tsp.	20 mL
Salt	1 tsp.	5 mL
Cooking oil	⅓ cup	75 mL
Milk	1 cup	250 mL

Mix first 4 ingredients together in bowl.

Add oil and milk. Stir to moisten. Form into a ball. Press into greased 9 x 13-inch (22 x 33 cm) pan, forming sides about ½ inch (1½ cm) high. May also be baked in small pie plates.

FILLING

Sauerkraut, rinsed and drained 3 times	14 oz.	398 g
Corned beef, flaked (or 2 small tins)	12 oz.	341 g
Shredded Swiss cheese	1½ cups	375 mL
Mayonnaise	⅔ cup	150 mL
Chili Sauce	⅓ cup	75 mL
Sweet pickle relish	2 tbsp.	30 mL
Dry onion flakes	1 tbsp.	15 mL

Measure all ingredients into bowl. Mix well. Spread over crust. Bake in 400°F (200°C) oven for 25 to 30 minutes until browned. Serve warm, cut into squares. Serves 15-18 as a sit-down appetizer or cut into smaller squares for finger food.

Pictured on page 117.

SCOTCH EGGS

An age-old recipe from Great Britain.

Sausage meat	1 lb.	500 g
Hard-boiled eggs	8	8
All-purpose flour	1 tbsp.	15 mL
Egg, beaten	1	1
Dry bread crumbs, rolled fine	1 cup	250 mL

Fat for deep-frying

Divide sausage meat into 8 equal portions. Roll out each portion. Dust eggs thoroughly with flour, then wrap each egg with meat. Dampen hands with cold water for easier handling.

Dip each into beaten egg, then roll in crumbs. Deep-fry in 375°F (190°C) fat until well browned. Serve hot or cold. May be halved or quartered. May also be baked in greased pan in 450°F (225°C) oven for 20 minutes or until browned. Serve hot or cold with or without mustard sauce for dipping. Makes 32 tidbits.

MUSTARD SAUCE

Mayonnaise	½ cup	125 mL
Prepared mustard	1 tbsp.	15 mL

Mix together. Transfer to dipping bowl. Serve as a dip for Scotch Eggs and other foods.

When peeled, these eggs have a marbled appearance.

Eggs	10	10
Water to cover		
Soy sauce	½ cup	125 mL
Tea bags	2	2
Salt	1½ tsp.	7 mL
Water	3 cups	750 mL
Cinnamon (optional — adds flavor)	1 tsp.	5 mL

Put eggs into saucepan. Cover with water. Bring to boil. Simmer, covered, for about 12 minutes. Drain. Cover with cold water and drain a few times until water stays cold. Drain. Crack each shell gently all over with a tablespoon or by rolling gently. Do not remove shells.

Combine soy sauce, tea bags, salt, water and cinnamon in large saucepan. Add eggs. Bring to boil. Simmer, covered, for 45 minutes. The eggs should be brown at this point. Remove from heat. Let eggs stand, covered, in liquid for at least 3 hours or 2-3 days. Remove shells, cut in halves or quarters to serve. Eggs will keep in juice in refrigerator for about 1 week. Makes 40 sections.

Pictured on page 117.

If you don't like her driving, keep off the sidewalk.

DEVILLED EGGS

One of the more substantial snacks.

Hard-boiled eggs	6	6
Salad dressing	¼ cup	50 mL
Dry mustard	½ tsp.	2 mL
Salt	½ tsp.	2 mL
Pepper	⅛ tsp.	0.5 mL
Paprika		

Cut eggs in half lengthwise. Put yolks on plate. Add salad dressing, mustard, salt and pepper. Mash with fork until smooth and mixed well. If too dry, add a bit of milk. Fill egg white halves. A pastry tube will give an artistic design.

Sprinkle with paprika. Makes 12.

Note: If using cooked salad dressing on page 135 in Company's Coming — Salads, omit mustard.

CAVIAR EGGS: Sprinkle with black caviar. Caviar may be tossed lightly with a bit of lemon juice and grated onion before sprinkling.

CURRIED EGGS: Mash ¼ tsp. (1 mL) curry powder with yolks.

PICKLED EGGS

It is easy to keep a supply of these on hand.

Hard-boiled eggs	12	12
Medium onion, sliced into rings	1	1
Vinegar	1 cup	250 mL
Water	1 cup	250 mL
Granulated sugar	¼ cup	50 mL
Whole cloves	8-10	8-10

Place cooled, shelled eggs into 1-quart (1 L) jar. Add onion rings.

Put remaining ingredients into saucepan. Bring to boil, stirring often. Remove from heat. Cool. Pour over eggs. Brine must cover eggs. Store, covered, in refrigerator for 1 week before eating. Makes 12.

RED PICKLED EGGS: Substitute beet juice for the water.

These are mouth-watering morsels to nibble on.

**Cheese — your favorite kind, cut
  into ½-inch (1 cm) cubes or shape
  into balls
Egg, beaten
Dry bread crumbs, finely rolled
  (or corn flake crumbs)**

Fat for deep-frying

Dip cheese cubes into egg, then coat well with crumbs. Dip in egg again followed by another coating of crumbs.

Deep-fry in hot fat 375°F (190°C) for 20 to 30 seconds until light brown. Drain on paper towels. Serve hot. These may be made ahead and reheated in 400°F (200°C) oven for about 5 minutes until hot. Cheese may be frozen before deep-frying if preferred. Make as many or as few as desired.

When Cinderella was told for the third time that her films hadn't been developed, she sighed "Some day my prints will come".

SHRIMP COCKTAIL

A special beginning for a special dinner. A family tradition.

Crisp lettuce, shredded	1½ cups	375 mL
Small or medium shrimp, rinsed and drained	4 oz.	113 g
Chili sauce	¾ cup	150 mL
Lemon juice	2 tsp.	10 mL
Worcestershire sauce	¼-1 tsp.	1-5 mL
Onion powder	½ tsp.	2 mL
Salt	¼ tsp.	1 mL
Peeled and diced apple	½ cup	125 mL
Finely chopped celery	¼ cup	50 mL

Line sherbet glasses with lettuce. Divide shrimp among sherbets, saving a few for garnish if desired.

Mix remaining ingredients in bowl, using smallest amount of Worcestershire sauce. Add until the right amount for you is reached. Spoon over shrimp shortly before serving. Serve with 2 small crackers placed beside each cocktail. (Ritz is good). Makes 4-5.

Variation: Omit apple. Double amount of celery.

Pictured on page 135.

SHRIMP BALL

Consider your heart won when you sample this. Expect rave reviews.

Mayonnaise	½ cup	125 mL
Butter (not margarine)	½ cup	125 mL
Cans of broken shrimp, drained	2 × 4 oz.	2 × 113 g
Minced onion	1 tbsp.	15 mL
Garlic powder	⅛ tsp.	0.5 mL
Lemon juice	1 tbsp.	15 mL
Parsley, chopped		
Paprika		

(continued on next page)

Cream mayonnaise and butter. Add shrimp, onion, garlic powder and lemon juice. Mix and form into ball, or pack into small plastic-lined bowl to remove later. Butter firms more than margarine when chilled and that is a requirement in this recipe.

Sprinkle with parsley and paprika. Chill. Serve with crackers, toast cups or flatbread. Makes about 2 cups (500 mL).

SHRIMP SPREAD: An easy alternative. Omit parsley and paprika, then press into dish for serving.

Pictured on cover.

CRABBY SNOW PEAS

It is hard to decide whether these are showier or tastier.

Snow peas, frozen (or fresh)	6 oz.	170 g
Crab	4¾ oz.	135 g
Hard-boiled egg, chopped	1	1
Mayonnaise	2 tbsp.	30 mL
Finely chopped celery	2 tbsp.	30 mL
Finely chopped green onion	1 tbsp.	15 mL
Prepared mustard (Dijon is best)	¼ tsp.	1 mL

Slit thawed peas open on top side, which is the least curved side. If using fresh pods, pour boiling water over them, let stand for 10 seconds. Drain. Rinse with cold water until cold. Drain and keep cool.

Remove membranes from crab. Mix crabmeat with egg, mayonnaise, celery, onion and mustard. Stuff each pea pod until it looks like it is overflowing — about 1 tsp. (5 mL). Chill. Makes 2½ dozen.

Pictured on page 135.

SALMON FINGERS

A great way to present salmon or whatever your fishing catch may be.

Eggs	2	2
Milk or water	½ cup	125 mL
All-purpose flour	1 cup	250 mL
Cornstarch	2 tbsp.	30 mL
Baking powder	2 tsp.	10 mL
Seasoned salt	2 tsp.	10 mL
Salt	1 tsp.	5 mL
Salmon, boneless	1 lb.	454 g
All-purpose flour		

Fat for deep-frying

Beat eggs in bowl. Mix in milk. Add flour, cornstarch, baking powder, seasoned salt and salt. Stir well.

Cut salmon into medium-sized fingers. Dust with flour. Dip in batter and deep-fry. Drain on paper towels. Serve with Curried Tartar Sauce and Seafood Sauce, see page 22, for dipping. Serves 8-10.

CURRIED TARTAR SAUCE

Mayonnaise	1 cup	250 mL
Pickle relish	2 tbsp.	30 mL
Curry powder	¼ tsp.	1 mL

Mix together. Makes a good fish dip.

FISH STICKS: Use your favorite fish instead of salmon.

Pictured on page 135.

How come opportunity rarely knocks but temptation pounds away every day?

Scallops in shells double as a main dish but when served in smaller portions they make an elegant, sit-down appetizer. Simple to make ahead.

Butter or margarine	2 tbsp.	30 mL
Scallops, cut up	¾ lb.	350 g
Lemon juice	1 tbsp.	15 mL
Butter or margarine	2 tbsp.	30 mL
Sliced mushrooms	½ cup	125 mL
Green onion, chopped	1	1
White wine	¼ cup	50 mL
Butter or margarine	2 tbsp.	30 mL
All-purpose flour	2 tbsp.	30 mL
Salt	½ tsp.	2 mL
Pepper	⅛ tsp.	0.5 mL
Milk (half cream is better)	1 cup	250 mL
Paprika	⅛ tsp.	0.5 mL
Bread crumbs, dry	3 tbsp.	50 mL
Butter or margarine, melted	2 tsp.	10 mL
Grated Parmesan cheese	¼ cup	50 mL

Combine butter and scallops in frying pan. Sauté for about 2 minutes. Stir in lemon juice. Divide among coquilles (shells).

Put second amount of butter into frying pan. Add mushrooms and onions. Sauté until tender. Stir in wine. Boil until wine is half boiled away. Transfer to small bowl. Set aside.

Put third amount of butter into frying pan. Stir in flour, salt and pepper. Add milk stirring to thicken. Add paprika. Add mushroom mixture. Mix together. Taste to check whether more salt is needed. Spoon over scallops.

Toss bread crumbs with melted butter. Scatter over top. Sprinkle with cheese. Bake in 400°F (200°C) oven for 15 to 20 minutes until browned. Makes 6 appetizers.

Note: Substitute apple cider for the wine if you prefer.

Variation: Shredded Cheddar or Gruyère may be used instead of Parmesan.

Variation: Mashed potatoes may be piped around outside edge of scallops before baking. It has the added advantage of making the serving look larger.

Although this makes a large quantity, your guests will eat several, so be prepared.

Ground pork	¾ lb.	375 g
Shrimp, chopped	½ lb.	250 g
Finely chopped water chestnuts	½ cup	125 mL
Finely chopped green onions	½ cup	125 mL
Soy sauce	1 tbsp.	15 mL
Salt	½ tsp.	2 mL
Wonton wrappers	1 lb.	454 g

Lard or cooking oil for deep-frying

In medium-sized bowl mix pork and shrimp. Add water chestnuts, onion, soy sauce and salt. Mix together well.

Put about ½ tsp. (3 mL) in center of wonton wrapper. Since these brown very quickly, too much filling won't have time to cook. Moisten edges, fold over to form triangle. Press edges to seal. Fold 2 corners over, moisten and press together to seal.

Deep-fry in 375°F (190°C) fat until golden brown. Drain on paper towels. Serve hot with Apricot Sauce, see page 80, or sauce of your choice. Makes 7-8 dozen.

Note: May be reheated by placing on baking sheet. Heat in 350°F (180°C) oven for 10 minutes or until heated through. They may also be frozen raw in single layers then bagged. Thaw before deep-frying.

Pictured on page 135.

SHRIMP BALLS

Shape filling into balls. Roll in flour or cornstarch and deep-fry in 375°F (190°C) fat.

When the whole crowd likes oysters, have them sit up to the table for this great beginning to any meal.

Oysters, chilled and raw, on half shell
Brown bread or rolls
Lemon wedges
Tabasco sauce

Place oysters on small plates. Set thin buttered bread strips or roll beside oysters on plates. Pass lemon wedges and Tabasco. Allow 2 to 3 oysters per serving.

Note: To shuck oysters, hold scrubbed oyster over a bowl, to catch the oyster liquor. Pry oysters open at hinge end, with oyster knife, turning knife to cut through hinge muscle. Cut oysters off shell, rinse, return to shell and strain liquor over oyster.

ANGELS ON HORSEBACK

For oyster lovers.

Oysters	12	12
Lemon juice sprinkle		
Cayenne pepper sprinkle		
Chopped parsley	2 tbsp.	30 mL
Bacon slices, half-cooked, sliced in half crosswise	6	6

Sprinkle oysters with lemon juice, cayenne and parsley. Roll in bacon, securing with wooden pick. Place on baking tray. Bake in 400°F (200°C) oven for 5 to 10 minutes until bubbling hot and bacon is cooked. Serve hot. Makes 12.

Variation: Smoked oysters may be used rather than regular ones.

ESCARGOTS

A special treat for snail lovers.

Escargots (1 can)	24	24
Butter or margarine	⅔ cup	150 mL
Parsley flakes	1 tsp.	5 mL
Garlic powder	½ tsp.	2 mL
Onion powder	½ tsp.	2 mL
Salt	¼ tsp.	1 mL
Pepper	⅛ tsp.	0.5 mL
Parmesan cheese, grated		

Clean snails in cold water. Put into pan or casserole.

Melt butter in small saucepan. Add parsley, garlic powder, onion powder, salt and pepper. Stir to mix. Spoon over top of snails.

Sprinkle liberally with Parmesan cheese. Bake uncovered in 350°F (180°C) oven for about 5 minutes or until heated through. Serve in escargot dishes with or without the shells. Serves 4-5.

ESCARGOT-STUFFED MUSHROOMS: Place 1 snail in each hot mushroom cap.

GLAZED SHRIMP

These are colorful little bites that glisten. Different and good.

Cold water	1¼ cups	300 mL
Unflavored gelatin	¼ oz.	7 g
Ketchup	½ cup	125 mL
Vinegar	1 tsp.	5 mL
Celery salt	½ tsp.	2 mL
Shrimp, cocktail-size	4¼ oz.	120 g

Measure water into saucepan. Sprinkle gelatin over top. Let stand 5 minutes. Heat and stir over medium heat until dissolved.

Stir in ketchup, vinegar and celery salt. Remove from heat. Allow to cool until you can hold your hand on saucepan.

(continued on next page)

Drain shrimp well. Blot dry with paper towel. Dip in gelatin mixture. Put on plates. Chill to set. Dip second time. Chill. This gives a better glaze. Serve on small crackers or small toast squares. Serves 8-10.

GLAZED SARDINES: Use sardines instead of shrimp. Serve on toast points.

SCALLOPS WITH BACON

A gourmet treat that disappears in no time.

Bacon slices	6	6
Scallops	12	12

Cut bacon slices in half crosswise. Fry slowly until partially cooked. Do not fry too much or it will not be soft enough to roll when cool. Remove from pan. Cool.

Cook scallops in enough boiling water to cover. Boil 5 minutes. Drain. Cut large scallops in half. Cool.

Roll bacon around scallop. Secure with toothpicks. To serve, arrange on baking pan. Heat in 425°F (220°C) oven for about 10 minutes until bacon is sizzling hot and scallops are heated through. Serve hot. Makes 12 appetizers.

Note: Uncooked bacon may be used to wrap cooked scallops. Broil for about 5 minutes. Turn and broil 5 minutes more.

Pictured on page 135.

If you own an owl and a goat, you have a hootenanny.

CRAB ROLLS

These are earthly delights.

Velveeta cheese	¼ lb.	125 g
Butter or magarine	¼ cup	50 mL
Can of crab	5 oz.	142 g
Salt	⅛ tsp.	0.5 mL
Pepper	1/16 tsp.	0.5 mL
Loaf of white sliced bread	1	1
Butter or margarine, melted		

Put cheese and butter into saucepan. Melt over low heat. Add crab, salt and pepper and mix well. Remove from heat.

Remove crusts from bread slices. Using rolling pin, roll each slice quite thin. Spread with crab mixture. Roll up jelly roll style. Chill or freeze.

To serve, brush with melted butter. Slice each roll into 3 pieces. Place on ungreased baking sheet. Bake in 400°F (200°C) oven for about 15 minutes until toasted. Makes 48.

LOBSTER ROLLS: Use lobster instead of crab. Delicious.

CRAB LOGS

An easy make-ahead snack, cooked from the frozen state.

Crab, drained	4¾ oz.	135 g
Dry bread crumbs	1 cup	225 mL
Tomato sauce or juice	½ cup	125 mL
Parsley flakes	1 tsp.	5 mL
Lemon juice	2 tsp.	10 mL
Horseradish	1 tsp.	5 mL
Egg	1	1
Salt	¼ tsp.	1 mL
Pepper	1/16 tsp.	0.5 mL
Bacon slices, half-cooked and cut in half crosswise	12	12

(continued on next page)

Put crab into bowl. Remove membrane. Add crumbs, tomato sauce, parsley, lemon juice, horseradish, egg, salt and pepper. Mix together well. Shape into 24 short log-shaped rolls.

Wrap with bacon. Secure with toothpick. Put single layer on baking sheet to freeze. Store in plastic bag. To serve, broil frozen logs 4 inches (10 cm) from heat for about 5 minutes, turning at half time, until golden brown. Will take about 10 minutes if bacon was not precooked. May also be baked (providing bacon was precooked) in 400°F (200°C) oven for about 10 minutes until sizzling. Serve hot. Makes 24.

SEAFOOD APPETIZER

For your most special dinner. Keep a piece of frozen barbecued salmon on hand as it isn't always readily available. Scrumptious little kabobs. Serve when money is no object.

Scallops	12	12
Barbecued salmon chunks	12	12
Medium shrimp, fresh or canned	12	12
Short wooden skewers	6	6
Butter or margarine	½ cup	125 mL

Cut large scallops in half. Carefully cut salmon into chunks. If salmon is frozen, thaw completely to avoid crumbling. Thread on skewer, 1 scallop, 1 chunk salmon, 1 medium shrimp, 1 scallop, 1 chunk salmon, 1 medium shrimp. Arrange in square baking pan.

Put pan over low heat. Put butter into pan and heat until melted. Baste seafood. Put in 375°F (190°C) oven and baste several times with butter adding more if needed. This will take about 10 minutes or so. Transfer 1 skewer to each plate. Serve hot to 6 lucky people.

BROILED SEAFOOD KABOBS: Mushroom caps, bacon squares, pineapple chunks and green pepper chunks may be added or exchanged. Broil 3 or 4 inches from heat. Turn for even cooking.

SHRIMP TEMPURA

Exotic company fare.

All-purpose flour	¾ cup	175 mL
Cornstarch	¼ cup	50 mL
Baking powder	1 tsp.	5 mL
Salt	1 tsp.	5 mL
Cold water	¾ cup	175 mL
Egg	1	1
Large fresh shrimp (see note)	2 lbs.	900 g

Fat for deep-frying

Measure flour, cornstarch, baking powder and salt into bowl. Mix.

Beat water and egg together slightly in small bowl with a spoon. Pour into flour mixture. Stir to mix.

Holding shrimp by the tail, dip into batter then drop into 375°F (190°C) fat. Turn once. Remove when browned. Serve with Mustard Sauce, page 116, Apricot Sauce, page 80, or Pineapple Sauce, page 23.

Note: Remove shells, leaving tail. Remove dark vein from back of shrimp. Cut inside curve of shrimp but not all the way through. Spread flat. This is a butterfly shrimp. Using tail as a handle, dip in batter. Drop in 375°F (190°C) fat and fry. Makes about 3 dozen.

People fight for the right to say what they think, then they say too much without thinking.

These can be held in the refrigerator and deep-fried at the last minute or they can be deep-fried ahead of time and reheated at the last minute. Either way, you will need to make lots.

Crab	4 ¾ oz.	135 g
Cream cheese, room temperature	8 oz.	250 g
Green onions, finely chopped	2	2
Salt	¼ tsp.	1 mL
Wonton wrappers	1 lb.	454 g

Fat for deep-frying

In medium-sized bowl mix crab with cream cheese. Add onion and salt. Mix well.

Place 1 tsp. (5 mL) in center of wonton wrapper. Moisten edges. Fold over, forming triangle. Press edges to seal. Fold 2 corners over, moisten and press together to seal.

Deep-fry a few at a time, turning to brown both sides, in hot fat 375°F (190°C). Drain on paper towels. Serve immediately or cool and store in covered container in refrigerator with waxed paper between layers.

To serve, arrange on baking sheet. Heat in 350°F (180°C) oven for about 15 minutes until hot. Good with Sweet and Sour Sauce, page 77, Plum Sauce page 23, Apricot Sauce, page 80. Makes 4 to 5 dozen.

Note: Uncooked wontons may be frozen in a single layer, then bagged. Thaw before deep-frying.

Pictured on page 135.

A shaking ship is apt to end up on the ocean floor as a nervous wreck.

LAYERED CRAB SPREAD

Worth breaking any diet for.

Cream cheese, softened	8 oz.	250 g
Sour cream	½ cup	125 mL
Mayonnaise	¼ cup	50 mL
Worcestershire sauce	2 tsp.	10 mL
Dry onion flakes	2 tsp.	10 mL
Chili sauce	¾ cup	175 mL
Canned crab, membrane removed	2 × 4¾ oz.	2 × 135 g
Shredded mozzarella cheese	2 cups	500 mL
Paprika		
Parsley		

Mix first 5 ingredients. Spread over 12-inch (30 cm) pizza pan.

Spread chili sauce over cheese. Layer crab then cheese evenly over top. Sprinkle with paprika. Garnish with parsley. Cover and chill. Serve with crackers. Serves 8-10.

LOBSTER SPREAD

This versatile spread goes a long way. Definitely a class act!

Lobster, mashed	5 oz.	142 g
Hard-boiled eggs, chopped	2	2
Finely chopped celery	1 tbsp.	15 mL
Dry onion flakes, crushed	½ tsp.	2 mL
Salad dressing	1 tbsp.	15 mL

Combine all ingredients. Spread on your favorite crackers. Use as stuffing for tiny cream puff shells or cherry tomatoes. Makes about 1 cup (250 mL).

SURPRISE SPREAD

You will be tempted to eat this no-bake spread by the spoonful.

Cream cheese, softened	8 oz.	250 g
Sour cream	½ cup	125 mL
Mayonnaise	¼ cup	50 mL
Cans of small or broken shrimp, rinsed and drained	3 × 4 oz.	3 × 113 g
Seafood cocktail sauce	1 cup	250 mL
Shredded mozzarella cheese	2 cups	500 mL
Green pepper, chopped	1	1
Green onions, chopped	3	3
Tomato, diced	1	1

Mix first 3 ingredients together. Spread over 12-inch (30 cm) pizza pan.

Scatter shrimp over cheese mixture. Add layers of seafood sauce, mozzarella cheese, green pepper, onions and tomato. Cover and chill until ready to serve. Supply assorted crackers and spoons for spreading. Toast cups are great. Serves 10-12.

Note: Omit 1 can of shrimp if desired. It will still cover quite well.

Pictured on page 135.

SPREADING FOREST FIRE

This is a quick bean dip. A natural for corn chips.

Beans in tomato sauce, drained and mashed	14 oz.	398 mL
Grated sharp Cheddar cheese	1 cup	250 mL
Butter or margarine	½ cup	125 mL
Very finely chopped onion	½ cup	125 mL
Garlic, powder	¼ tsp.	1 mL
Salt	¼ tsp.	1 mL
Pepper	⅛ tsp.	0.5 mL
Hot pepper sauce	½ tsp.	2 mL

Put all ingredients into heavy saucepan. Heat, stir until melted. Serve warm with corn chips and tortillas. Makes 3 cups (750 mL).

Note: A few slices of jalapeño peppers, ground, may be substituted for the hot pepper sauce. Then you really will have a fire!

ANTIPASTO

Use some, freeze some — be prepared always.

Finely chopped cauliflower	1 cup	250 mL
Ripe olives	1 cup	250 mL
Finely chopped green olives	¼ cup	50 mL
Chopped pickled onions	½ cup	125 mL
Cooking oil	¼ cup	50 mL
Mushroom pieces, drained and chopped	10 oz.	284 mL
Small green pepper, finely chopped	1	1
Ketchup	2¼ cups	550 mL
Sweet mixed pickles, finely chopped, juice reserved	12 oz.	341 mL
Finely chopped red pepper (optional)	¼ cup	50 mL
Sweet pickle juice	3 tbsp.	50 mL
Tuna, drained	7 oz.	198 g
Broken or tiny shrimp, drained	4 oz.	113 g

Put first 5 ingredients into large saucepan. Bring to boil over medium heat. Simmer 10 minutes.

Add next 6 ingredients. Return to boil. Simmer 10 minutes more. Stir often.

Add tuna and shrimp. Stir. Chill. Serve with party crackers, toast cups, etc. Makes 6 cups (1.5 L).

Variation: Use dill pickles rather than sweet.

If you put a bunch of ducks in a box, would you really have a box of quackers?

BLUE CHEESE BALL

You may not care for blue cheese but this is sure to be an exception. Just the right tang.

Cream cheese, softened	8 oz.	250 g
Grated sharp Cheddar cheese	2 cups	500 mL
Blue cheese	4 oz.	113 g
Butter or margarine	¼ cup	50 mL
Onion flakes, crushed	1 tsp.	5 mL
Garlic powder (or 1 clove, minced)	¼ tsp.	1 mL
Finely chopped nuts	⅔ cup	150 mL
Chopped parsley (optional)	¼ cup	50 mL

Combine first 6 ingredients in bowl. Mix well. Shape into ball or if you prefer, into 2 balls.

Roll in nuts, or if you are using parsley too, mix nuts and parsley together first, then roll. Chill until about 1 hour before using. Leftovers may be reshaped into a ball again and frozen for future use. Supply spreading knives and assorted crackers. Makes about 3 cups (750 mL).

PINEAPPLE CHEESE BALL

Mellow green pepper flavor blends with the pineapple to produce yet another good cheese ball.

Cream cheese, softened	2 x 8 oz.	2 x 250 g
Crushed pineapple, well drained	½ cup	125 mL
Pecans, chopped (optional)	1 cup	250 mL
Dry onion flakes, crushed	2 tsp.	10 mL
Chopped green pepper	¼ cup	50 mL
Seasoned salt	2 tsp.	10 mL
Finely chopped pecans	½ cup	125 mL

Cream cheese until soft and smooth. Add next 5 ingredients. Mix well. Shape into ball.

Roll in pecans. Chill. Serve with crackers. Makes about 3½ cups (875 mL).

ONION CHEESE BALL

All the seasoning comes from the soup mix. Good onion flavor.

Cream cheese, softened	8 oz.	250 g
Grated sharp Cheddar cheese	2 cups	500 mL
Sour cream	1 cup	250 mL
Walnuts, finely chopped	½ cup	125 mL
Envelope dry onion soup mix	½ × 1½ oz.	½ × 42.5 g
Finely crushed soda crackers	½ cup	125 mL
Walnuts, finely chopped	½ cup	125 mL

Beat cream cheese, Cheddar cheese and sour cream until soft and smooth. Mix in nuts, onion soup and cracker crumbs.

If too soft to shape into a ball, chill awhile, then shape it. Roll in nuts. Freezes well. Makes 4 cups (1 L).

BEST CHEESE BALL

When someone has the courage to cut into this beauty, it will quickly be sampled by everyone.

Cream cheese, room temperature	2 x 8 oz.	2 x 250 g
Shredded sharp Cheddar cheese	2 cups	500 mL
Worcestershire sauce	2 tsp.	10 mL
Onion flakes	1 tsp.	5 mL
Lemon juice	1 tsp.	5 mL
Cayenne pepper	⅛ tsp.	0.5 mL
Salt	⅛ tsp.	0.5 mL

Pecans or walnuts, finely chopped.

Measure first 7 ingredients into bowl. Mash and mix together. Shape into ball.

Roll in nuts. Put cocktail knives and crackers nearby so guests can dig right in. Leftovers may be reshaped, rewrapped and frozen if not going to be used within a week. Makes about 3¼ cups (875 mL).

Variation: Add 1 tbsp. (15 mL) chopped green pepper and 1 tbsp. (15 mL) chopped pimiento. Tiny balls are attractive.

Pictured on cover.

A stunning red-shelled dip.

Edam cheese, room temperature	1 lb.	455 g
Cream cheese, softened	8 oz.	250 g
Butter or margarine	¼ cup	50 mL
Sour cream	¼ cup	50 mL
Mayonnaise	¼ cup	50 mL

Draw a pattern, scalloped or zig-zag, a little smaller than top of cheese. Use it as a guide to cut off top. Using spoon or melon baller, scoop out cheese, leaving shell intact. Grate or chop cheese into fine pieces.

Put cheese pieces in blender along with remaining ingredients or use beater. Blend together well adding more mayonnaise if needed to obtain soft consistency. Spoon most of filling into shell, using the rest for a refill. Serve with toast points, crackers or flat bread. Serves 10.

STUFFED GOUDA: Use Gouda cheese instead of Edam. Just as delicious.

Pictured on page 27.

A good way to fancy-up this soft cheese.

Small round Camembert cheese	1	1
Cream cheese, softened	4 oz.	125 g
Orange juice	1 tbsp.	15 mL
Sliced almonds	2 tbsp.	30 mL
Grapes, seeded, peeled and sliced	2 tbsp.	30 mL

Cut Camembert cheese in half to look like a layered cake.

Mash cream cheese with orange juice. Mix in almonds and grapes. Reserving 1 tbsp. (15 mL), spread rest of mixture over bottom layer of cheese. Put top layer over filling. Smooth reserved spoonful over top. Goes well with Welsh Cakes, page 33. Serves 8.

LIPTAUER CHEESE BALL

An excellent version of a cheese that was originally made from sheep's milk.

Cream cheese, softened	8 oz.	250 g
Butter or margarine, softened	½ cup	125 mL
Sour cream	¼ cup	50 mL
Caraway seeds	1 tsp.	5 mL
Dry onion flakes, crushed	1 tsp.	5 mL
Prepared mustard	1 tsp.	5 mL
Salt	¼ tsp.	1 mL
Garlic powder	⅛ tsp.	0.5 mL
Pepper	⅛ tsp.	0.5 mL

Paprika
Parsley (optional)

Beat cheese, butter and sour cream until smooth. Mix in caraway seeds, onion flakes, mustard, salt, garlic powder and pepper.

Shape into ball, chilling first if necessary. Dust with paprika. Add parsley for garnish if you wish. Makes 1⅔ cups (400 mL).

Variation: Four anchovies, chopped, may be added to ingredients before shaping into ball.

It was impossible to play cards on the Ark with Noah always sitting on the deck.

CHILI CHEESE LOG

You will need to make this three or four days ahead to mellow.

Grated Cheddar cheese	3 cups	750 mL
Cream cheese, softened	4 oz.	125 g
Worcestershire sauce	¾ tsp.	3 mL
Garlic salt	½ tsp.	2 mL
Pepper	¼ tsp.	1 mL
Chili powder	lots	

Put Cheddar cheese, cream cheese, Worcestershire sauce, garlic salt and pepper into mixing bowl. Beat until soft and smooth. Roll into 2 rolls. Make diameter a bit smaller than round cracker so slices will fit on top.

Sprinkle waxed paper liberally with chili powder. Roll to coat each log well. Wrap in waxed paper. Chill in refrigerator for 3 or 4 days to blend. Put slices on round crackers or serve with a cheese knife and assorted crackers. Freezes well. Makes 4-5 dozen slices.

Pictured on page 81.

CURRIED CHEESE SPREAD

Delicious. Good on anything!

Cream cheese, softened	8 oz.	250 g
Apricot jam	¼ cup	50 mL
Chopped almonds or cashews, toasted	⅓ cup	75 mL
Curry powder	¼-½ tsp.	1-2 mL
Dry mustard	¼ tsp.	1 mL

Mash cheese and jam together. Mix in nuts, curry powder and mustard. Add smaller amount of curry first then more if needed. Pack in small bowl. Serve with butter knife and crackers. Makes about 1¼ cups (300 mL).

CURRIED CHEDDAR SPREAD: Substitute 2 cups (500 mL) grated sharp Cheddar cheese for the cream cheese.

CHUTNEY SPREAD: Substitute chutney for the apricot jam.

Note: Toast almonds in 350°F (180°C) oven for about 10 minutes until browned. Stir once or twice.

BRIE EN CROÛTE

The cheese is baked inside the pastry and served hot. Impress your company. Regular pastry may also be used.

Frozen puff pastry, thawed
Small Brie cheese

Roll out pastry fairly thinly on lightly floured surface. Put cheese on pastry. Cut around cheese making pastry circle a bit larger than the cheese. Cover cheese with more pastry, sealing around bottom edge. Bake on ungreased baking sheet in 425°F (220°C) oven for 10 to 15 minutes until golden brown. Brushing crust with some beaten egg gives a shiny finish. Serve hot with crackers. Serves 6-8.

CAMEMBERT EN CROÛTE: Use a Camembert round instead of Brie. Makes a great impressive spread.

HAM AND CHEESE BALL

It is easy and convenient to have all of the makings on hand for this good spread.

Cream cheese, softened	8 oz.	250 g
Cans of ham flakes	2 × 6½ oz.	2 × 184 g
Dried chives	2 tsp.	10 mL
Lemon juice	2 tsp.	10 mL
Worcestershire sauce	½ tsp.	2 mL

Parsley, chopped

Beat or mash cheese and ham together until blended. Add chives, lemon juice and Worcestershire sauce. Shape into ball, chilling first if necessary. If too soft, shape into mound on plate.

Roll in parsley. Chill. Serve with crackers. Makes 2½ cups (575 mL).

HAM ROLL CANAPÉS: Form into a roll. Make roll smaller in diameter than your favorite round cracker. To serve, place thin slices on crackers, or use as a spread.

POLYNESIAN CREAM CHEESE

Not only is this quick and easy, but a block of cheese may be cut in half lengthwise to make two varieties.

Cream cheese	**8 oz.**	**250 g**
Soy sauce	**⅓ cup**	**75 mL**
Sesame seeds, toasted	**1-2 tbsp.**	**15-30 mL**

Put block of cream cheese into small bowl or plastic bag. Pour soy sauce over top. Marinate 1 hour. Remove cheese to serving plate. Pour more soy sauce over if needed.

Sprinkle with seeds using more if desired. Cheese may also be rolled in seeds, using enough to cover. Serves 6.

ORIENTAL CHEESE SPREAD: Marinate in Teriyaki sauce or use ½ cup (125 mL) soy sauce with ¼ cup (50 mL) granulated sugar. Roll in ⅓ cup (75 mL) toasted sesame seeds. Sprinkle any leftover seeds on top.

Note: Toast sesame seeds in 350°F (180°C) oven for about 5 minutes, stirring once or twice, until browned.

MEXICAN CHEESE SPREAD: Spoon salsa over top of block of cream cheese in shallow dish.

APRICOT CHEESE SPREAD: Mix ¼ cup (50 mL) apricot jam, ½ tsp. (2 mL) hot pepper sauce and 2 tsp. (10 mL) cider vinegar. Pour over block of cream cheese.

CHUTNEY BACON SPREAD: Put cream cheese in center of pretty plate. Spoon ¼ cup chutney over top letting it run down sides. Sprinkle with 6-8 slices cooked and crumbled bacon.

SAUCED CHEESE SPREAD: Pour your favorite steak sauce over block of cream cheese. Sprinkle with toasted sesame seeds if desired.

SHRIMP CHEESE SPREAD: Pour seafood sauce or chili sauce over block of cream cheese. Arrange small, drained shrimp over top.

CRAB CHEESE SPREAD: Mix seafood sauce or chili sauce with contents of a tin of crabmeat (remove membranes). Spoon over block of cream cheese letting it run down sides.

SEEDED CHEESE SPREAD: Roll cream cheese block in caraway seeds, poppy seeds or crushed nuts.

CORNED BEEF MOUSSE

An easy-to-make spread that is absolutely luscious.

Cold water	¼ cup	50 mL
Unflavored gelatin	¼ oz.	7 g
Condensed cream of mushroom soup	10 oz.	284 mL
Cream cheese, softened	8 oz.	250 g
Curry powder	¼ tsp.	1 mL
Finely chopped onion	½ cup	125 mL
Finely chopped celery	½ cup	125 mL
Mayonnaise	1 cup	250 mL
Flakes of corned beef	6.5 oz.	184 g

Sprinkle gelatin over cold water in saucepan. Let stand for 5 minutes.

Add mushroom soup, cream cheese and curry powder. Heat and stir until dissolved and melted. Remove from heat. Chill until it begins to thicken.

Add onion, celery and mayonnaise. Break up corned beef and fold into mixture. Pour into mold. Chill. To serve, unmold on serving plate. Supply crackers, toast points or toast cups. Makes about 5 cups (1.1 L).

CRAB MOUSSE

So festive when served with tiny toast cups piled around. Supply a knife so guests can help themselves.

Cold water	¼ cup	50 mL
Unflavored gelatin	¼ oz.	7 g
Condensed cream of mushroom soup	10 oz.	284 mL
Cream cheese, softened	8 oz.	250 mL
Mayonnaise	⅔ cup	150 mL
Finely chopped celery	¾ cup	175 mL
Tin of crabmeat (or fresh)	5 oz.	142 g
Worcestershire sauce	1½ tsp.	7 mL
Dry onion flakes	1 tsp.	5 mL

(continued on next page)

Put cold water into medium saucepan. Sprinkle gelatin over top. Let stand for 1 minute.

Add mushroom soup, cheese and mayonnaise. Heat and stir until dissolved and melted. Remove from heat. Chill until it begins to thicken.

Add celery. Drain crab and remove membrane. Add crabmeat, Worcestershire sauce and onion. Stir well. Pour into ring mold or fish mold. Chill. To serve, unmold on serving dish. Surround with toast cups and/or crackers. Serves 15-20.

SALMON PÂTÉ

An inexpensive spread with expensive smoked salmon appeal.

Cream cheese, room temperature	4 oz.	125 g
Grated onion	2 tsp.	10 mL
Lemon juice	1 tsp.	5 mL
Horseradish	½-1 tsp.	2-5 mL
Salt	⅛ tsp.	0.5 mL
Liquid smoke	½ tsp.	2 mL
Canned salmon (red is best)	7½ oz.	213 g

Mash cream cheese with onion and lemon juice. Add lesser amount of horseradish, adding more at the last if desired. Mix in salt and liquid smoke.

Drain salmon. Remove round bones and dark skin if any. Add and mix well. If needed, add a bit of red food coloring for appearance. Chill a few hours before using. Serve with assorted crackers, toast points or toast cups. Makes about 1½ cups (375 mL).

SALMON BALL: Double recipe. Shape into ball. Roll in finely chopped pecans or walnuts, about ½ cup (125 mL). Top with parsley flakes. May also be rolled in a mixture of nuts and parsley.

SALMON LOG: Roll into logs a bit smaller than round crackers. Slice and place on crackers.

TUNA PÂTÉ

A well-known spread, still as good as it used to be.

Can of tuna, drained	7 oz.	198 g
Cream cheese, softened	4 oz.	125 g
Butter or margarine, softened	¼ cup	50 mL
Chopped onion	½ cup	125 mL
Lemon juice	1 tsp.	5 mL
Salt	⅛ tsp.	0.5 mL
Pepper	⅛ tsp.	0.5 mL
Finely chopped nuts (optional)	½ cup	125 mL

Measure all ingredients into blender. Blend until smooth. Or use a beater, beating until smooth. Pack into bowl. Chill. Serve with crackers. Garnish with parsley, chives or nuts. Makes 1⅔ cups (400 mL).

LIVER PÂTÉ

Simple to prepare, a tasty spread.

Chicken livers	¾ lb.	375 g
Water to cover		
Butter, room temperature	½ cup	125 mL
Finely chopped onion	3 tbsp.	50 mL
Sherry or fruit juice	3 tbsp.	50 mL
Dry mustard	1 tsp.	5 mL
Salt	½ tsp.	2 mL
Nutmeg	¼ tsp.	1 mL
Cloves	⅛ tsp.	0.5 mL
Pepper	⅛ tsp.	0.5 mL
Cayenne	⅛ tsp.	0.5 mL

Put livers and water into saucepan. Bring to boil. Cover and simmer for about 20 minutes. Drain. Grind livers in food chopper or use blender.

Add remaining ingredients. Mix until smooth. Mound mixture on plate or spoon into oiled mold. Chill. Serve with cocktail knives or butter spreaders and cocktail crackers. Makes a generous 2 cups (500 mL).

#1

Place filling in center. Moisten edges.	Fold over to make triangle. Press to seal.	Fold 2 corners to center. Moisten and press to seal.

#2

Place filling in center. Moisten edges.	Fold over to form rectangle. Press to seal.	Twist ends.

#3

 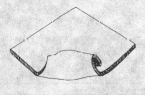 

Place filling in 1 corner. Moisten edges.	Tuck corner around filling.	Fold side corners in like an envelope.

Roll over once more.	Turn flap down to seal.

EGG ROLL WRAPPING: same as #3

CUTTING PATTERNS

For meat stacks, canapés, etc.

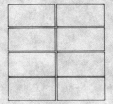

8 oblongs

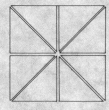

8 triangles

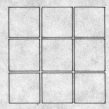

9 squares

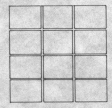

12 oblongs

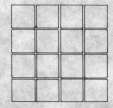

16 squares

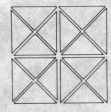

16 triangles

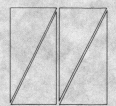

4 toast points

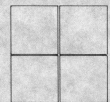

toast squares

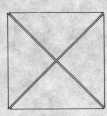

toast triangles

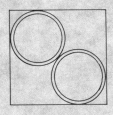

2 bread rounds

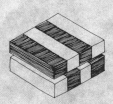
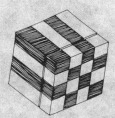

checkerboard sandwiches

Throughout this book measurements are given in Conventional and Metric measure. To compensate for differences between the two measurements due to rounding, a full metric measure is not always used. The cup used is the standard 8 fluid ounce. Temperature is given in degrees Fahrenheit and Celsius. Baking pan measurements are in inches and centimetres as well as quarts and litres. An exact metric conversion is given below as well as the working equivalent (Standard Measure).

OVEN TEMPERATURES

Fahrenheit (°F)	Celsius (°C)
175°	80°
200°	95°
225°	110°
250°	120°
275°	140°
300°	150°
325°	160°
350°	175°
375°	190°
400°	205°
425°	220°
450°	230°
475°	240°
500°	260°

SPOONS

Conventional Measure	Metric Exact Conversion Millilitre (mL)	Metric Standard Measure Millilitre (mL)
1/4 teaspoon (tsp.)	1.2 mL	1 mL
1/2 teaspoon (tsp.)	2.4 mL	2 mL
1 teaspoon (tsp.)	4.7 mL	5 mL
2 teaspoons (tsp.)	9.4 mL	10 mL
1 tablespoon (tbsp.)	14.2 mL	15 mL

CUPS

1/4 cup (4 tbsp.)	56.8 mL	50 mL
1/3 cup (51/3 tbsp.)	75.6 mL	75 mL
1/2 cup (8 tbsp.)	113.7 mL	125 mL
2/3 cup (102/3 tbsp.)	151.2 mL	150 mL
3/4 cup (12 tbsp.)	170.5 mL	175 mL
1 cup (16 tbsp.)	227.3 mL	250 mL
41/2 cups	1022.9 mL	1000 mL (1 L)

DRY MEASUREMENTS

Ounces (oz.)	Grams (g)	Grams (g)
1 oz.	28.3 g	30 g
2 oz.	56.7 g	55 g
3 oz.	85.0 g	85 g
4 oz.	113.4 g	125 g
5 oz.	141.7 g	140 g
6 oz.	170.1 g	170 g
7 oz.	198.4 g	200 g
8 oz.	226.8 g	250 g
16 oz.	453.6 g	500 g
32 oz.	907.2 g	1000 g (1 kg)

PANS, CASSEROLES

Conventional Inches	Metric Centimetres	Conventional Quart (qt.)	Metric Litre (L)
8x8 inch	20x20 cm	12/3 qt.	2 L
9x9 inch	22x22 cm	2 qt.	2.5 L
9x13 inch	22x33 cm	31/3 qt.	4 L
10x15 inch	25x38 cm	1 qt.	1.2 L
11x17 inch	28x43 cm	11/4 qt.	1.5 L
8x2 inch round	20x5 cm	12/3 qt.	2 L
9x2 inch round	22x5 cm	2 qt.	2.5 L
10x41/2 inch tube	25x11 cm	41/4 qt.	5 L
8x4x3 inch loaf	20x10x7 cm	11/4 qt.	1.5 L
9x5x3 inch loaf	23x12x7 cm	12/3 qt.	2 L

INDEX

If you don't see Company's Coming where you shop, ask your retailer to give us a call. Meanwhile, we offer a mail order service for your convenience.

Just indicate the books you would like below. Then complete the reverse page and send your order with payment to us.

Buying a gift? Enclose a personal note or card and we will be pleased to send it with your order.

Deduct $5.00 for every $35.00 ordered.

See reverse.

Company's Coming
COOKBOOKS®

Companys Coming Publishing Limited
Box 8037, Station F
Edmonton, Alberta, Canada T6H 4N9
Tel: (403) 450-6223

MAIL ORDER COUPON

QUANTITY • HARD COVER BOOK •

Jean Paré's Favorites - Volume One

TOTAL $17.95 + $1.50 shipping = **$19.45 each** x [ ] = $ [ ]

TOTAL BOOKS / TOTAL PRICE

QUANTITY • SOFT COVER BOOKS •

ENGLISH

150 Delicious Squares	Pasta
Casseroles	Cakes
Muffins & More	Barbecues
Salads	Dinners of the World
Appetizers	Lunches
Desserts	Pies
Soups & Sandwiches	Light Recipes
Holiday Entertaining	Microwave Cooking
Cookies	
Vegetables	
Main Courses	

TOTAL $10.95 + $1.50 shipping = **$12.45 each** x [ ] = $ [ ]

TOTAL BOOKS / TOTAL PRICE

QUANTITY • PINT SIZE BOOKS •

Finger Food
Party Planning
Buffets

TOTAL $4.99 + $1.00 shipping = **$5.99 each** x [ ] = $ [ ]

TOTAL BOOKS / TOTAL PRICE

QUANTITY • SOFT COVER BOOKS •

FRENCH

150 délicieux carrés	Recettes légères
Les casseroles	Les salades
Muffins et plus	La cuisson au micro-ondes
Les dîners	Les pâtes
Les barbecues	
Les tartes	
Délices des fêtes	

TOTAL $10.95 + $1.50 shipping = **$12.45 each** x [ ] = $ [ ]

TOTAL BOOKS / TOTAL PRICE

Please fill in reverse side of this coupon

TOTAL PRICE FOR ALL BOOKS
*(See reverse) ** $ [ ]

COOKBOOKS

Companys Coming Publishing Limited
Box 8037, Station F
Edmonton, Alberta, Canada T6H 4N9
Tel: (403) 450-6223

MAIL ORDER COUPON

TOTAL PRICE FOR ALL BOOKS (from reverse)	$
Less $5.00 for every $35.00 ordered	- $
SUBTOTAL	$
Canadian residents add G.S.T.	+ $
TOTAL AMOUNT ENCLOSED	$

Gift Giving

We Make It Easy...You Make It Delicious

Let us help you with your gift giving! We will send cookbooks directly to the recipients of your choice if you give us their names and addresses. Be sure to specify the titles of the cookbooks you wish to send to each person.

Send the Company's Coming Cookbooks listed on the reverse side of this coupon to:

Name:

Street:

City: Province/State:

Postal Code/Zip: Tel: (   )   —

Company's Coming Cookbooks make excellent gifts. Birthdays, bridal showers, Mother's Day, Father's Day, graduation or any occasion... collect them all! Remember to enclose your personal note or card and we will be pleased to send it with your order.

If you don't see Company's Coming where you shop, ask your retailer to give us a call. Meanwhile, we offer a mail order service for your convenience.

Just indicate the books you would like below. Then complete the reverse page and send your order with payment to us.

Buying a gift? Enclose a personal note or card and we will be pleased to send it with your order.

Deduct $5.00 for every $35.00 ordered.

See reverse.

SAVE $5.00!

Companys Coming Publishing Limited
Box 8037, Station F
Edmonton, Alberta, Canada T6H 4N9
Tel: (403) 450-6223

MAIL ORDER COUPON

QUANTITY • HARD COVER BOOK •

		TOTAL BOOKS	TOTAL PRICE
	Jean Paré's Favorites - Volume One		

TOTAL $17.95 + $1.50 shipping = **$19.45 each** x ⬜ = $⬜

ENGLISH

QUANTITY • SOFT COVER BOOKS •

150 Delicious Squares		Pasta	
Casseroles		Cakes	
Muffins & More		Barbecues	
Salads		Dinners of the World	
Appetizers		Lunches	
Desserts		Pies	
Soups & Sandwiches		Light Recipes	
Holiday Entertaining		Microwave Cooking	
Cookies			
Vegetables		TOTAL BOOKS	TOTAL PRICE
Main Courses			

TOTAL $10.95 + $1.50 shipping = **$12.45 each** x ⬜ = $⬜

QUANTITY • PINT SIZE BOOKS •

Finger Food			
Party Planning		TOTAL BOOKS	TOTAL PRICE
Buffets			

TOTAL $4.99 + $1.00 shipping = **$5.99 each** x ⬜ = $⬜

FRENCH

QUANTITY • SOFT COVER BOOKS •

150 délicieux carrés		Recettes légères	
Les casseroles		Les salades	
Muffins et plus		La cuisson au micro-ondes	
Les dîners		Les pâtes	
Les barbecues			
Les tartes		TOTAL BOOKS	TOTAL PRICE
Délices des fêtes			

TOTAL $10.95 + $1.50 shipping = **$12.45 each** x ⬜ = $⬜

Please fill in reverse side of this coupon   **TOTAL PRICE FOR ALL BOOKS** $⬜
(See reverse) *

Deduct $5.00 for every $35.00 ordered.

COOKBOOKS

Companys Coming Publishing Limited
Box 8037, Station F
Edmonton, Alberta, Canada T6H 4N9
Tel: (403) 450-6223

MAIL ORDER COUPON

TOTAL PRICE FOR ALL BOOKS (from reverse)	$
Less $5.00 for every $35.00 ordered −	$
SUBTOTAL	$
Canadian residents add G.S.T. +	$
TOTAL AMOUNT ENCLOSED	$

• **ORDERS OUTSIDE CANADA:**
  Must be paid in U.S. funds by cheque or money order drawn on Canadian or U.S. bank.

• *Prices subject to change without prior notice.*

• *Sorry, no C.O.D.'s*

• **MAKE CHEQUE OR MONEY ORDER PAYABLE TO:**
  COMPANY'S COMING PUBLISHING LIMITED

Gift Giving

We Make It Easy...You Make It Delicious

Let us help you with your gift giving! We will send cookbooks directly to the recipients of your choice if you give us their names and addresses. Be sure to specify the titles of the cookbooks you wish to send to each person.

Send the Company's Coming Cookbooks listed on the reverse side of this coupon to:

Name:

Street:

City: _____ Province/State:

Postal Code/Zip: _____ Tel: (_____) _____ — _____

Company's Coming Cookbooks make excellent gifts. Birthdays, bridal showers, Mother's Day, Father's Day, graduation or any occasion... collect them all! Remember to enclose your personal note or card and we will be pleased to send it with your order.